everything
I would
have said

STEPHANIE WEICHERT

everything I would have said

SURVIVAL STRATEGIES FOR GETTING THROUGH TOUGH TIMES

ISBN: 978-0-578-55313-9

Library of Congress Control Number: TXu 2-154-312

Front cover and book design by Damonza.com
Headshot on back cover by JohnDortonPhotography.com

Printed by IngramSpark in the United States of America.

First printing edition 2019.

Sarahson Publishing
Brentwood, TN, 37027

www.stephanieweichert.com

To my small tribe who loved me through some of my darkest moments and to the one who really needs the encouragement. This book is for you.

CONTENTS

FOREWORD

By: Ken Weichert (SGT Ken®)

AS A COUNTERINTELLIGENCE Agent during Operation Iraqi Freedom, rapport was one of the best strategies that I employed. Rapport means to find common ground. It also means that what is important to the person in front of you should always be important to you. This is how we form our deepest connections, an ongoing process that has the potential to enrich and empower one's life. In my case, while serving in Iraq, it may have saved mine.

My favorite source in Iraq was a man named Hassan, a simple farmer who did his best to help me keep his small village as safe as possible. The information he provided more often than not led to the incarceration of bad guys or the capture of weapons caches. He considered it doing his part to give democracy a fighting chance.

After several months of working with Hassan, the soldiers that lived on my base trusted him sufficiently enough to allow him to enter without an escort. He simply showed up, signed in, and walked through the gate, right past the armed guards.

This could be both good and bad.

At one point during my deployment, our task force had been on the hunt for Saddam Hussein and we had not slept in three days. We decided to take a break from the mission and get back to our sleeping quarters for some much-needed rest. But first I needed to type an intelligence information report while the information was still fresh in my mind.

At the time, I was living in a small shelter that I shared with my translator, Sam, a husky Egyptian-American noncombatant who snored louder than anyone I've ever met. Between the fatigue of not sleeping for three days, and Sam's loud snoring, I could not type a single comprehensible sentence.

I decided to give it a break. I closed my laptop and laid my head down for what would be my first sleep in 72 hours. After about 20 minutes, I was wakened by a faint noise.

When I opened my eyes I noticed a moving shadow and immediately realized an intruder had entered our shelter. As the adrenaline surged through my body, I reached underneath my pillow and grabbed my combat knife. By now the intruder had moved close to me and was breathing hot air into my face. I was just about to lunge forward when a voice cried out, "It's so terrible! It's so terrible!" I recognized the voice and held back. Then I flicked on a small light to see who it was that I had nearly killed.

It was Hassan, my farmer friend, desperate to share something that was burdening his heart. Sam stopped snoring and I watched his eyes pop open. "Help me translate," I asked him.

"I'm not translating anything," he said in perfect English while eyeing Hassan. "He's stupid." Sam was aware of the social pecking order that existed in the Middle East and felt Hassan was beneath his efforts.

I looked back at Hassan, whose face was puffy and red with hot tears. Between my elementary Arabic and Hassan's even worse English, we did our best to communicate.

I remembered that what was most important for me to focus on was what was important to the person in front of me. That is how I had earned trust and built relationships in that small community, and particularly, with Hassan.

The people in the Middle East speak with long, flowery sentences.

To better connect with them, I always matched their speech patterns and rhythms. "Hassan, you have traveled so far in the deepest part of the night, your heart weighs heavy, your sandals worn thin, to tell your friend, Mr. Ken, something that weighs you to the ground."

Clearly in despair he responded with, "Yes, yes, yes."

I still didn't know why he was sitting in front of me on the floor.

Finally Hassan blurted out, "My goat is missing!" I wondered if I had misunderstood him. I was waiting for "and I think my neighbor is planning to kill me" but it didn't come. His goat was missing and he was upset. End of story. In my fatigue, I wanted to shout a few expletives and raise an American-style, middle finger salute. But I held back.

Sam broke his silence. In a sing-song voice he said, "I told you."

"Quiet, Sam," I said sharply then turned to Hassan. Though his missing goat wasn't at the top of my list of concerns, I knew better than to tell him that. What was called for in this situation was empathy. And that became the opening Hassan needed to reveal his deeper concern.

The goat milk meant income. With the goat missing, he would not be able to provide for his small family. What to me was a simple case of an AWOL farm animal, to him was a matter of life and death. I racked my brain for a solution to his plight. Then something occurred to me. "Hassan, isn't your brother also a goat farmer?"

"Yes," said Hassan. He lifted his head out of his hands and stopped crying.

"Could it be that your favorite goat has wandered off to your brother's farm?"

Hassan's countenance completely shifted, and a glimmer of hope entered his eyes.

He immediately left and went to his brother's farm. I learned later that my theory had been correct. There, among his brother's herd, he found his wayward, prized goat.

A couple of weeks later Hassan showed up with credible

information about an attack that was being planned against our base that same night. His intelligence included specific details about how, and who, would be carrying it out.

A Special Forces team hastily set up an observation post near where the alleged attack would take place. Just as Hassan had described, at 2105 hours, there was a flash in the night sky from the mortar that was propelled from the back of the flatbed of a Toyota pickup truck. But because we had advance knowledge of the attack we were able to thwart it and in so doing prevent a potentially catastrophic loss of lives.

All because I paused and listened to a man tell me about his favorite goat, and he returned the gesture with kindness.

The connection that Hassan and I formed in wartime was profound. According to Stephanie Weichert, the connections you form in your daily life are no less significant. "Connection is lifeblood," she writes in this book, which was inspired in part by a tragic incident in her past that was the result of a missed connection.

Thankfully for us, Stephanie is the kind of person who not only can absorb the slings and arrows life directs at her, she sees the pain as a teacher. This life-affirming book is a result of everything she's learned—a concise roadmap by a seasoned traveler down life's sometimes bumpy path, filled with the joy of sharing what she knows and where she's been, gentle support for those just starting out, and specific guidance for navigating the roadblocks, obstacles and emotional tangents that can bog you down or prevent you from reaching your final destination: embracing your authentic self, perhaps the most important connection of all.

I am extremely grateful to have worked with Stephanie at Warrior Fit Camp for the Tennessee Army National Guard. Her courage, candor, and commitment helped numerous soldiers and airmen find healing and happiness. She is a consummate professional that I call a colleague, companion, and best friend.

Enjoy the journey.

THE REASON I FINALLY SAT DOWN TO WRITE THIS BOOK

EARLY IN MY career, I worked for a major fitness corporation in downtown San Francisco. The company was full of high-energy people. There was one in particular who always stood out—Trevor. His ultra-calm demeanor was atypical for the fitness industry. He had the gift of hospitality and a magnetic personality. I always felt at ease around him. His down-to-earth nature would neutralize the busyness-hangover that the city produced.

Trevor and I were promoted to management at the same time. I began managing a slightly dilapidated former community center known for its basketball courts. He was given a coveted location in one of the trendiest neighborhoods in the city.

When the company decided to close my club, I was transferred to a higher-volume club that had been managed by Trevor and he was moved to a renovated club where my husband, Ken, taught boot camp fitness classes on Monday and Wednesday nights.

When I came into Trevor's club to take my husband's class, Trevor would be there to greet me with a warm smile. He was a sincere and genuine person. His kindness made time stand still. I always forgot about the chaos of the day once I made it in the front door of his club.

Somehow, I'd always imagined Trevor's life to be the epitome of perfection.

Trevor outlasted me as a general manager. I left the company to pursue a different career and eventually moved to a quiet little village of townhouses in the East Bay. After the move, I stopped taking my husband's class at Trevor's club. A couple of years later, my husband and I moved to Nashville, Tennessee, and Trevor and I lost touch.

Months later, I received a Facebook message from a woman I didn't know, who turned out to be Trevor's mom. Although I'd seen a few peculiar posts on Trevor's page, they hadn't truly registered. Now, his mother confirmed my vague, unfocused concerns: Trevor had committed suicide. Trying to make sense of his death, his mother had written to ask me if Trevor had contacted me before he took his life. Apparently, she knew from Facebook that I had done suicide prevention work for the Army National Guard, and Trevor had once told her he would contact me for life coaching.

But he never did. And now he was gone.

This is when I became deeply moved to finish the book I'd wanted to write—this book. I'd previously written the first thousand words, but didn't fully commit to completing it until after Trevor's death, when I had an experience that made me realize I needed to write it—to honor his life and to help others in similar situations.

That experience came in the form of a dream. I dreamt about a real-life fatherly figure named Karl, and a large group of people at a warm cabin in the middle of the cold, dark woods. Karl's wife, children, and grandchildren were all there. While his family was visiting with the other guests, people he had helped over the course of his life began showing up in the dream. I had conversations with a few of them.

Everyone was nearly moved to tears as each person gave their testimony of what Karl had done, or was currently doing, in their lives. Each of them mentioned that without him, none of their success would have been possible. It would have taken far too long, cost too much money, or extended beyond what they were capable of without his assistance. Because he had been generous, both personally and professionally, his encouragement had literally given these specific individuals what they needed to move forward in life.

Then, at one point, he sat down to play the piano. One of his friends sat on his right on the piano bench, harmonizing with every song he played. Karl played the chords while his friend played the melody. Somehow, the music carried an inspirational, hope-filled message.

After waking up from that dream, I began pondering the deeper meaning. I had a revelation: The melody that Karl and his friend created was a metaphor for how being engaged in the moment creates harmony that produces transformation in and around us. It's as though our chords of kindness, contribution, and love are met with a synchronistic melody from the Eternal one, and when combined, they make a deep impression on other people's lives. We do this when we become emotionally alive and not afraid to contribute the piece of us that makes us special.

For Karl, his song reached the people in his hometown. Others may have a smaller or larger platform. Each of us has a platform. It might be as small as the people in our own home, or we may go on to be well known throughout the world. The number of people is irrelevant. Being brave and touching the life of even one person with our unique gift is enough. Being brave starts with being known. Being known requires us to show others the contents of our soul.

The part that grieves me the most about Trevor, and anyone who lives with a cloud of depression or lack of hope, is that their melody grows dull. We can be alive and emotionally dead. When we come alive and allow for connection, we water the soil of our soul, where the seeds of our unique melody have been planted since the day we were born. When we choose to play, it's as though there's a partnership with others—and, I believe, with the Creator—that creates a spiritual harmony that's carried through future generations.

Our song becomes our lasting legacy. No one else can sit down to finish our melody. It starts and stops with each of us, individually.

When Trevor died, his music stopped. He was never able to finish his symphony. It was as though the pianist walked away from the concerto. The chords he had yet to play were left unexpressed, unheard, and never reached their full manifestation. What Trevor didn't realize was that his love, his work, his kindness, his individual fingerprint on the world was a unique song that would end with his death. When he died, so did the manifestation of his destiny. His destiny was to impact the world, perhaps starting with his own child.

Through the sadness, I had to ask myself: What would I have said to Trevor if he had called? What could I say to other people in Trevor's position, trying to keep their heads above water as they battle personal struggles? Many of us go through seasons of seemingly insurmountable problems, such as employment issues, relationship struggles, financial setbacks, or health crises, any of which may lead to feelings of isolation and worthlessness.

Everything I Would Have Said is born of these life experiences. It's a practical guide for reinventing your life by moving away from isolation, anxiety, and sadness, toward a courageous, hope-filled life. And it's also intended as a beacon for those seeking a new season of hope, connection, and purpose. This book includes heartfelt conversations with my coaching clients at various points in their lives, which I'm using with permission. Although many of them are in the fitness industry, their stories and problems are universal. *Everything I Would Have Said* demonstrates the step-by-step process for ending self-defeating patterns once and for all, and delivers a practical roadmap to finding fulfillment today.

There are plenty of self-help books out there; *Everything I Would Have Said*, however, peels back the curtain for a glimpse at just how many people are struggling to find a sense of worthiness, significance, and purpose. Throughout the pages, you'll be given a "me too" perspective on big issues. By seeing how common these issues really are, and reading about empowering steps to overcome them, you'll be inspired to move forward and keep going.

BE EMPOWERED

It's common knowledge that the first step to achieving a bountiful life is ending one's patterns of pain. The negative mindsets we adopt throughout our lives eventually begin to dissolve our hope and endurance, and science has proven, time and again, that a self-defeating attitude is the primary roadblock on the path to success.

Often this mindset is caused by a harsh upbringing or a traumatic experience of some sort. The narrative my coaching client Lucas had created for himself, for example, was built on perceived inadequacies. It wasn't until we started applying the methods in this book that he was able to move out of a self-defeating mental state and into a positive, forward-moving one. We worked together to construct a fresh core belief and to lose the "scarcity mindset" in order to change his ultimate story.

Everything I Would Have Said empowers each of us to take the same steps as Lucas in our own lives. Are strategies a cure for a problem? No, I don't think they are. Tools unscrew, they tighten, and they hammer in. Over time, everyone needs a little fine-tuning.

Once the negative mindset is identified, it's important to develop real-time resilience to dead-end thinking patterns and habits, and to change that inner dialogue. Once we understand our triggers, we can begin to change our emotional reactions to them. Starting from a macro perspective, then switching to micro perspective, we will learn how to implement these new ideals on a daily basis. In addition to continuing to follow the journey of Lucas and others who have gone through this process, we will discover a four-step model for conscious redirection. These are tools to help move us back to connection, back to peace, and back to fulfillment.

It's important to not only identify what isn't working, but to also learn how to move forward meaningfully after pain and defeat. It's necessary to learn how to connect and leave ourselves open to new experiences. This book identifies a process for moving forward, and, as our relationships with one another are some of the most defining aspects of our lives, I place a focus on overcoming issues that hold us back from forming beneficial ones.

Lastly, *Everything I Would Have Said* delves into learning how to "play your song" and rise from pain to purpose—how to discover your deepest intention, align your life with those values, and take action, despite the possibility of failure. We will discover how to determine if our actions are supporting our values, how to overcome excuses, and how to take these concepts and use them as guiding principles. In a bonus chapter by my husband, SGT Ken®, you will learn to build relationships through rapport.

I wish that Trevor had reached out to me when he was in need. I wish that I could have shared with him the lessons I've shared with my clients over the years. This book is for Trevor and for everyone else who's struggling to make their way in the world while fighting the negative voices inside. When we allow these voices to override the good and what's right with us, we stop showing up to play, and we lose the opportunity to connect with kindness, hope, and love. It's time, today, to get re-centered, and show the world the gift that has been locked away, inside.

FIRST LIFE LESSON: END THE PATTERN OF PAIN

SINGER-SONGWRITER RANDY PHILLIPS wrote a song titled, "Tell Your Heart to Beat Again." The inspiration for the song was a story he'd heard about a woman, Mrs. Johnson, who was to undergo heart surgery.[1] As the story goes, her surgeon was a member of an Ohio congregation whose pastor asked the doctor if he could watch the surgery.[2] The pastor liked adventure. He was known to skydive, do bungee jumping and ride motorcycles. For him, it would be exciting to witness a major surgery.

The doctor agreed, and the pastor was present in the operating room. But what ultimately peaked his interest wasn't the procedure after all. It was what happened afterward. The surgeon, having stopped the patient's heart for the surgery, used routine techniques to get her heart to "wake back up" afterward. When the blood starts flowing back through the heart, it should naturally resume beating.[3]

That day, Mrs. Johnson did not experience the norm. Despite the doctor following all medical steps to resuscitate her heart, it didn't respond. Worried, he reached into her chest and began massaging her heart with his hands.

Still no beat.

There was nothing more he could do medically. Her heart would have to resume beating on its own or she would die on the operating table.

Time was of the essence, so the doctor decided to try something that fell outside of medical protocol. He knelt down next to Mrs. Johnson's still body and spoke to her, believing she could hear him.

"Mrs. Johnson, this is your surgeon," he said. "The operation went perfectly. Your heart has been repaired. I need you to tell your heart to beat again."

Then the doctor stood up, and he and the pastor watched the heart monitor. Although Mrs. Johnson was still unconscious, the monitor began to register a pulse. She told her heart to beat again, and it did.

There is a moment many of us face after tough times—a choice to emotionally die on the operating table and live a small life, where we stay hidden and closed off from pain. We may have sought help to get through such trying times, but can't seem to regain a sense of balance. We get stuck in patterns that create feelings of worthlessness, numbness and isolation. In order to regain the life-giving flow we need to heal, we have to make a decision to step out into new, uncharted territory. This section is about recognizing the cycles so we can break them.

Chapter One introduces the cycles that keep us stuck. Chapter Two explores how we use dead-end patterns of thinking that dissolve hope. In Chapter Three, we discover how our narrative may have rendered us powerless. In this section, we will learn that, though we may have started with a harsh upbringing or a traumatic experience, it's never too late to begin to build positive, hope-filled, inspiring experiences into our lives.

No extra stimulus or motivational force can make it happen.

We have to tell our heart to beat again. It's our choice. And it's an important endeavor, because someone is waiting for you—for each of us—to come alive. Our music wasn't meant to simply entertain—it was meant to heal souls and deliver hope.

The concert hall is silent without our music.

. . . .

References

1. Danny Gokey "Tell Your Heart To Beat Again" Behind The Music. (2016, March 02). Retrieved February 03, 2017, from http://www.air1.com/music/news/2016/03/02/danny-gokey-tell-your-heart-to-beat-again-behind-the-music.aspx

2. Phillips, Craig & Dean - "Tell Your Heart To Beat Again" Story Behind The Song [R. Phillips Interview]. (n.d.). Retrieved February 03, 2017, from https://www.youtube.com/watch?v=pdPp7ofeBMA&feature=youtu.be
Fair Trade Services Youtube page

3. What To Expect During Heart Surgery. (2013, November 08). Retrieved February 03, 2017, from https://www.nhlbi.nih.gov/health/health-topics/topics/hs/during

CHAPTER ONE

STRATEGY #1: CONSTRUCT A FRESH CORE BELIEF

"If you are going through hell, keep going."

—Winston Churchill

MY SON WAS 3 when I first saw him do his happy dance. I can't remember why he did it—I think it was something he did naturally.

It began as just a quick shuffle when he felt spontaneously joyful. Later, he would indulge us by request. "Do the happy dance!" my husband would say. Our son obliged with a rousing jig in the middle of the kitchen.

At the drop of a hat, energy emanated out of his very core, into his arms, legs and face. He would laugh and smile during his happy dancing moments. His joy was infectious. He spread it wherever he went. He would sprinkle a little in the kitchen. He would happy dance in the aisles at Costco. Wherever he did his dance, everyone around him became cheerful, too.

Since he was born, my husband and I have tried to fill our son's "tank" with a sense of worthiness, through statements like, "I love you." "You're special." "You belong." "You amaze me." He hears these words every single day. But even he didn't continue the happy dance past the age of 7.

At some point, each of us experiences fractures, holes or a crushing of our tank—our reservoir of worthiness. Life sends a message that pierces our sense of well-being, and the tank leaks. Then, when problems arise, we have no reserves from which to draw. When our tank is low, our sense of personal value is low, and we begin to isolate—to stop connecting with others. We stop believing in ourselves. We stop hoping. We stop dreaming that things will improve.

For the boys at the Children Attitude Motivational Program (C.A.M.P.) hosted by the Counter-drug Force, Tennessee National Guard in Smyrna, TN, the result of their crushing was undesirable behavior. But, though their behavior had become a problem, the real problem was that their tanks were empty.

Is your tank empty? Do you need hope? Keep reading.

CHILDREN'S ATTITUDE MOTIVATIONAL PROGRAM

The weeklong program known as C.A.M.P., held at an armory near Nashville, Tennessee, included 100 boys ages 12—17. They were there for a variety of behavioral problems, such as drugs, alcohol and grand theft—they were out of control. The program was designed to help them make better choices and stay out of jail, through physical fitness activities and lectures on topics such as resilience, conflict resolution, life skills and drug prevention.

I was invited to address the group as a life coach.

The first year I spoke, I tried to inspire them. But it didn't work. I left with the sense that my message didn't penetrate their emotional armor. I felt my words fall to the ground as quickly as they were spoken. It was a good message that didn't take root. I had a hunch about why—probably something to do with my appearance and soft approach to storytelling. To them, I probably looked like just another speaker. Maybe even like their mom. How could I possibly have a message that would be important to them?

The next year, as I was preparing to speak there again, I decided to try something different. I needed the boys to get past me and get down to the core message. I decided to tell them my own story—what had initially damaged my self-esteem—so they could begin to relate my story to theirs.

They were from all parts of Tennessee. I recognized a few faces from the previous year, but most were new. They were weary, unkempt boys with shaved heads, divided up into counties by colored T-shirts. Enormous drill sergeants stood poised to yell at them if they did not sit up properly and at least appear to be listening. Occasionally, one of the guards would catch one of them tuning out during a lecture and would make him hold a squat with his back against the wall for several minutes.

They were a truly captive audience, and it was like trying to inspire people in a hostage environment. I knew they could hear me. Their eyes would remain open. Whether my words sank in was something entirely different.

I looked out at the sea of dirty, exhausted faces, and felt kindness and empathy toward them. I wanted to help them rise above their emotional wounds. I so wanted them to come away feeling inspired to change. I was worried that the protective emotional walls they'd built would keep them from embracing my message.

Trying to diffuse the physical tension in the room, I polled the kids. "Whose parents are on drugs?" I asked. Hands shot up. "Whose parents are divorced?" More hands. "Whose parents are in jail or prison?" A few more. By that time, the majority of the kids had raised their hands. One small, wide-eyed boy caught my attention. He didn't seem to belong there.

I silently prayed that my message might actually stick with them, and him in particular. They might forget me personally, but I wanted to spark an unquenchable fire of hope that would remain in their hearts long after they left the program. I wanted to help fill their tanks.

Before I began, I took a long pause to fully absorb the moment. My heart became heavy, burdened for them as they peered back at me. I reconnected with that hellish feeling from my youth, of hating my circumstances and having no power to fix them. I wanted to show them that change happens from the inside out—not the outside in. I knew I needed to stay focused, or I would see some of the same faces again next year.

"Who here knows who Robert Downey Jr. is?" A few kids raised their hands. "Who knows 'Iron Man'?" They all knew "Iron Man." I went on to tell them how the successful star of the movie was once heavily addicted to drugs for many years, but decided to change his life. "Your past does not determine your future," I told them. "Your choices determine your future."

Then I realized I needed to approach them on a deeper level. It suddenly seemed too easy to talk about choices, when their lives were filled with hardship. It was too much to ask them to do things differently, add some big goals to the mix, stir them together and wind up with a happy-dancing kind of life. To reach them, I had to engage their hearts. So I shared a painful story from my childhood. I knew it would pale in comparison to some of their experiences, but it was still pretty raw.

"When my dad got drunk in public," I began, "he was upbeat. But when he got drunk in the privacy of our home, which was most afternoons and evenings, he was angry and loud. When I wasn't being yelled at, I felt invisible and unimportant.

"When I was about 13, my dad used to take me to the races. He was friends with one of the car sponsors, so after the race, we would head to the pit for an after-party. There were kids of all ages milling around, also waiting for their parents. I stayed by them while my dad partied with the adults. One of those nights, as I stood around bored, I counted his empty Coors cans. There were nearly 20.

"A few hours later, when we were in his truck heading home, he was driving on the wrong side of the road. I remember sitting in silence, staring at the green digital clock, and thinking that if my dad was going to die driving, it would be best if I died too. I don't even know where the thought came from. It just showed up and hung like a heavy cloud.

"During the next few years of my life, every interaction I had with people started from that deficit. Hope had disappeared. I felt worthless. It wasn't about something anyone said to me—it's just something I started believing. From that one 30-minute drive, I built my story around an inner belief that I was a sad, insignificant person. And I based my perceptions about the world on that identity.

"In my childhood, my dad was more emotionally than physically abusive to me. He never hit me directly, but he threw me on the floor when the water boiled over on the stove, dragged me by the ear showing me dents and cracks in the paint—telling me they were my fault—and yelled at the top of his lungs, veins popping out of his neck, over the smallest things. It happened weekly. Sometimes, nightly.

"I wanted so badly to be accepted, approved of and loved. I was looking to him for that, but received only anger. I remember thinking I didn't belong anywhere—even in my own house. I believed something was wrong with me. I interacted with everyone from a sense of rejection and lack of value.

"Nothing—literally nothing—could fill that hole in my heart. I operated from a feeling of emotional poverty, and made all my choices from there."

I began to feel like I was connecting with the boys. Their expressions had changed a bit. Maybe their home life included physical violence. Maybe they were abandoned. The end result was the same: Our stories filled us with shame and made us feel worthless. They didn't seem to notice I was old enough to be their mom, now. They seemed fully engaged in the moment.

Still, I wondered what would become of them in a week, a month, five years from now. I wanted them to understand how our choices determine our future. I wanted to give them the sense that they had power over their lives. Their future didn't have to be shaped by the injustices and darkness they'd experienced. Their inherent value was not something anyone could take from them. It was theirs to keep—and to share.

I continued speaking, now feeling comfortable being completely vulnerable with them. You could have heard a pin drop.

"Who is to blame for my low self-esteem? Do I blame my dad? Or, should I blame his father? My grandfather was more abusive to my dad than my dad was to me. He mellowed out as he got older, but during my dad's formative years, he was very violent toward my dad. He would beat him until blood ran down his legs. And my dad, like me, was a just a small child looking for love and acceptance."

My dad's physical injuries healed, but his heart remained wounded. His childhood was so abusive that, even as an adult, hearing about it could make me cry. When he encountered any new struggles in his life, his tank was so empty that all he knew to do was numb it with alcohol and retaliate in anger.

I repeated my question to the young men. "Who is to blame for my terrible self-image? My father? My grandfather? How about his father—my great-grandfather? One day, taking my grandfather in the car on an errand, I learned that the physical violence went that far back—and beyond. 'This was just how things were done,' my grandfather told me. Neither parents nor children had language or permission to express hurt feelings back then. They just soldiered on.

"My grandfather's words reverberated through my mind. The cycle of 'how things were done' included violence, disconnection and emotional injury. Generationally, that side of my family never learned how to love well, which meant that each wounded person would wound the next.

"I broke the abuse cycle with my son, but I'd realize a few years later that I still hadn't plugged the hole in my tank. It was still leaking. I was still habitually reacting to life in survival mode and living in isolation. I still thought something was wrong with me. What I really needed was connection and to let love in. There *was* something wrong—but not with me as a child. As an adult, I had subconsciously embraced a dysfunctional thinking pattern. My actions stayed rooted in shame."

I paused and looked at them.

"Cycles tend to repeat themselves until they are intentionally broken," I said. "Like a domino effect, one bad decision can lead to another. If we aren't vigilant, we can take on other people's pain and pass it on to future generations."

Cycles begin with an inner belief. Negative cycles cause shame-based thinking—"something is wrong with me." To change the cycle, we need to make decisions based on a sense of personal value and the conviction that we are worthy of being loved. We need to seek relationships with empathetic, caring people. By forming deep bonds with such people, we can change our central beliefs. We learn that we deserve love. We begin to trust these new friends and confidantes. Trust creates intimacy. In the intimacy, we allow ourselves to be imperfectly perfect, and then our tank fills. Eventually, a sense of purpose flows from our faith to complete the things we have yet to accomplish.

The hard truth that I told the kids at C.A.M.P. that day was that instead of acting on the old, raw, hurt-filled emotions, we have to choose to believe a new truth.

"In about a week, you will all go back to the same situations you just came out of. If your parents were making bad decisions when you left, they'll still be making them when you go home. Your parents may not change, and you can't change them. But you're not responsible for their bad decisions. You are only responsible for your own."

Would my skeptical audience absorb that principle so deeply that their lives would be forever altered? I wasn't sure, but I had more to tell them about my journey.

"Although I recognized the cycle, my negative self-image didn't automatically disappear. I also had to identify and change my inner beliefs. So, each time old, negative feelings arose, I began to lovingly reaffirm my sense of significance and value. I worked on consciously stopping the shame-based cycle with deliberate, new actions.

"Moving forward, when approaching my dad, I needed to feel more like a self-assured person who wasn't looking to him to fill my tank. I had to stop responding to him from that wounded place. But it was very challenging. I kept anticipating his old behavior. I'd learned early on to appear emotionless, and I now had to become vulnerable enough to receive his positive efforts toward me.

"As I did so, the dynamic between us changed. The less I strived for love, the more freely he gave it. I accepted him as imperfect and readily forgave his mistakes. In turn, I let him see my own imperfections. It took the pressure off us both, and as he felt loved and accepted, he responded in kind."

I knew for many of these boys, their parents wouldn't change, and they would never get this opportunity. They would have to move through the process of healing and break the cycle without regard to their parents' actions. It was a tall order for a group of young kids.

I told the boys, "It was empowering when I realized I could only control what I decided to own. I could have remained bitter, angry and hurt— forgiveness was a choice I'd have to make. I also had to choose to believe I was valuable and lovable despite my flaws. When I did, I developed a sense of restoration that created a new foundation for my future—and it changed my life."

My story was messy. But I'm not alone. Many of us have messy pasts that left us with invisible scars. I wasn't a perfect person teaching the boys to be perfect. Rather, patching the hole in my tank was only the first step in my own healing process.

The young boy who had caught my attention earlier sat frozen in his seat. His eyes were filled with tears. At the close of the workshop, he was sobbing. As the others left the room, I invited him up to the front. "What's wrong?" I asked gently. In that moment, he seemed very small and timid. He was visibly shaking. It took several minutes before he could control the flood of emotions enough to answer me.

"I didn't... realize... I could... control... my future," he said in between sobs.

How many of us don't?

THE BELIEF EXPECTATION CYCLE

Many years ago, a pastor friend of mine outlined the Belief Expectation Cycle, a psychological behavior model created by a nonprofit organization called Restoring the Foundations®.[1] She explained how we experience a vicious cycle that causes us to re-experience negative emotions. Drawing a circle on a piece of scrap paper, the pastor showed me how the concept is divided into four distinct parts:

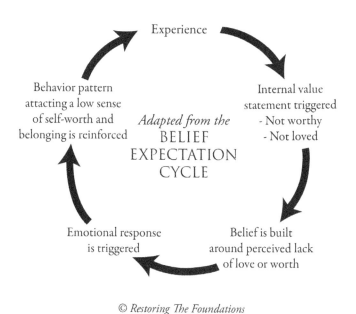

© Restoring The Foundations

The Belief Expectation Cycle creates a visual for how we relive painful experiences. The initial event leads to a belief about ourselves.

That belief leads to an expectation about our future. We unwittingly align our behavior with that expectation, and this causes us to unintentionally create new experiences that produce the same negative emotions we felt during the original incident.

The cycle continues unless interrupted.

The idea that I was recreating my negative childhood emotions was a foreign concept to me. I was an adult now and didn't have to do that. I was in control. Yet unconsciously, I was *choosing* the dysfunctional thinking originally caused by living with a raging alcoholic.

A poor self-image is self-perpetuating. Until *I* decided I mattered, people would continue to treat me as though I didn't. Until *I* began to believe I was acceptable, loved, and powerful, I looked for signs of disapproval, rejection, and reaffirmation of weakness.

These negative thinking patterns can cause us to hide from the world, lash out in anger, or numb our emotions through alcohol or drugs. We may stop reaching out and connecting with others. We repeat the choices that keep our tank empty. I had a daily decision to make.

Loving and approving of myself is that daily decision, and it has resulted in new behavior patterns and better interactions with people. I chose, and still choose, to affirm myself and belong. This results in connectivity, closeness, and positive emotion. I recognize when I'm slipping back into dysfunctional thinking, but I make the effort to correct course.

I showed the Belief Expectation Cycle to the boys that afternoon. Paraphrasing Kris Vallotton, Senior Associate Leader from Bethel in Redding, CA, I said, "We will recreate the reality that lives inside of us. If it's a reality that is based on an unstable foundation of no perceived value, we will inadvertently create a future with no perceived value. We will attract what we believe we are worth."

While we can't change our original experiences, we can change the beliefs they created by adopting new fundamental beliefs:

1. We are worthy no matter what happened to us or what we've done.
2. We are powerful and can make powerful decisions.
3. We are lovable despite how we sometimes feel.
4. We our capable of solving our current problem with patience and creative, new thinking.

No one else can fill our empty, cracked tank. A sense of significance is something we must first find within. When we do, we gain a quiet confidence that gives others permission to honor us the way we honor ourselves. It's a peace that comes from knowing we are loved, lovable, valued and valuable—that our identity is not defined by how people have treated us, our bad decisions, and/or our perceived lack of success.

Higher self-esteem begins with a new belief about ourselves. With this new belief comes a stronger sense of hope for the future. Then, we begin to make progress. We take the first vulnerable step, then the next.

WE ARE WORTHY OF BEING LOVED AND BELONGING

Let me make this personal: You are worthy of love and you matter. Your tank may feel completely crushed and dry, but you're important. *You have a purpose in life.* Your past does not have to dictate your future. However, it will probably be an influence until you become mindful of the Belief Expectation Cycle and decide to step out of it. Doing so takes a willingness to let things go and a decision to restore hope. It takes a conscious effort.

The first step in breaking the cycle is to stop thinking that other people, or things beyond our control, are responsible for our worth. No person or event will save us. We have to lovingly rescue ourselves. We have to learn how to operate from within the painful situation, and we begin by believing we are worthy—here and now.

- We are worthy when we are pursuing our dream career, in a transitional job we don't like, or if we haven't been able to keep a job.
- We are worthy whether our spouse affirms we are, or tells us we're not.
- We are worthy if we haven't found a life partner, or our life partner left us (or we left our life partner).
- We are worthy if we're sitting in prison waiting out a long sentence or sitting in our own home, isolated and full of despair.
- We are worthy whether we have children, or tried and couldn't, or never wanted any.
- We are worthy if we've been rejected or violated.
- We are worthy whether we're in perfect health or have a disease.
- We are worthy when we're wealthy or down to our last dollar.
- We are worthy if we've made a series of bad choices.
- We are worthy even if someone else told us we're not, or made us feel like we're not.

Feeling worthy is something we grow into. We do it by realizing we have the ability to change and move forward. Embracing that power is the first step out of the cycle. We are strong people with cracked tanks. But the cracks don't diminish our value. They make us human.

Powerful people take ownership of their lives. Rather than remaining stuck in our problems, we make decisions that lead to self-growth. We may start with a repetitive action, such as exercising, attending a 12-step program, or making a commitment to follow through on a new job. Even the smallest change can serve as a major force in helping us break out of negative patterns and rise from the ashes.

I believe (powerful people) share key characteristics. Although I will discuss each of these in later chapters, the following is a snapshot of a powerful person:

1. They have a positive way of thinking about themselves, resilience toward life's problems, and a healthy body and spirit. They're not perfect, but they continually work toward wellness and personal balance (Chapters Four, Five, and Six).

2. They have healthy connections and a sense of belonging. This means they allow their stories to be heard, but also have personal boundaries (Chapters Seven, Eight, and Nine).

3. They share their knowledge to make the world a better place. They know that their passions are meant to help bring love, kindness, beauty, healing, health, revelation, safety, ingenuity and so much more to a hungry world (Chapters Four, Ten, and Twelve), no matter how small the sphere of influence. They start with the one person in front of them.

4. Powerful people are able to name their feelings instead of calling themselves names. We all experience a broad range of emotions, including negative ones. Powerful people recognize this, and don't personalize the pain or let a condescending inner voice define their future (Chapters One, Three, and Six).

5. Powerful people aren't afraid to make major decisions. They start over when things don't work out as planned. They dig deep and try to live from a place of integrity every day (Chapters Two and Four).

6. Powerful people know that personal development is never complete. They work on improving themselves continually (the premise of the entire book).

✳ WHERE DO WE START? ✳

If we're going to embrace the idea that we're worthy and powerful, where do we start?

- We look for areas to improve upon.
- We look for chances to create life-affirming connections.
- We look for ways to make other people feel significant.
- We look for places to make a small difference.

These actions bring healing into the broken places, and help us realize we're powerful people with a purpose we haven't fully recognized yet. We discover that we're already equipped with the solution.

We must believe we're lovable and loved. Once we do, we can choose to move forward from our old story into a new journey.

Love says we're worthwhile. When we begin to believe we're lovable, we reclaim hope that our heart's deepest desires can come true. Learning to hope is a process and a choice. It's a way of thinking, a belief that the best is still ahead. If our mindset is based in hope, then, when we come upon obstacles, we recognize them for what they are and remember to return to that central core of optimism.

The fruit of living out of love instead of fear, hope instead of dread, is the belief that we can still achieve something great. Attaining greatness requires us to believe we're significant before we actually feel it. When we believe we're lovable, we can set goals and reach them, hope is reinforced, and a new story begins.

A hope-filled story says good things are in store for us.

Researcher and shame expert Dr. Brené Brown says, "We are neurologically and biologically hardwired for connection." We need others. When we allow others to love us, we can take the small steps that will change our lives. We can see things for what they really are. Our past does not have to define our future. More importantly, our story does not determine our past or future worthiness.

It's time to tell our heart to beat again.

HERE'S WHAT I WOULD SAY TO TREVOR AND TO YOU

You will need to see yourself as a worthy, lovable, and powerful person in order to stop the flow of dread, pain, and misery. Then you can create a new vision for yourself. This is a gift that no one can give you. You need to take it for yourself. When you do, you'll begin attracting the love and success your spirit needs to move forward.

Take a moment to think about a negative but significant event in your past, or something hurtful someone said to you.

You can use these questions for reflection:

1. What did you start, or stop, doing as a result of that event or those words?

2. If you believe your choices really determine your future, what new belief would you use to replace the old thought?

3. If something made you feel less than valuable, what is a new truth you could tell yourself?

To counteract negative thoughts, begin to think about what makes you special and unique. You also need to begin finding reasons you can achieve more in your life, instead of reasons you can't. Past events don't have to dictate your future. You are a special, worthy person. Your actions will be directly tied to whether or not you believe this core truth. It is your time to rise to a new place of worthiness. Your time to belong is now.

Love says we're worthwhile. When we begin to believe we're lovable, we reclaim hope that our heart's deepest desires can come true. Learning to hope is a process and a choice. It's a way of thinking, a belief that the best is still ahead. If our mindset is based in hope, then, when we come upon obstacles, we recognize them for what they are and remember to return to that central core of optimism.

• •

References

1. Kylstra, C., & Kylstra, B. (n.d.). [Belief Expectation Cycle, Restoring the Foundations Nonprofit Ministry].

CHAPTER TWO

STRATEGY #2:
LOSE THE SCARCITY MINDSET

"Too many people overvalue what they are
not and undervalue what they are."

—Malcolm S. Forbes

"WHERE WOULD YOU like to go with your session today?" I asked my new coaching client, Lucas.

He responded with, "That's a really good question. I've actually done a good deal of thinking about it."

Lucas was a young man in his early 20s who was born with a shoulder disability that would keep him from pursuing his deepest dream—a career in the military. Specifically, he hoped for a job in the Army Special Forces, on a Special Operations team, where he could help create and execute unconventional warfare strategies in waterborne, desert, jungle, mountain, or arctic operations.

Lucas would need a complete shoulder replacement for his arm to be fully functional, but the technology for that type of surgery had yet to be developed. Learning that the Army would never accept him was devastating to him, because he felt it meant he could never fulfill his potential.

Lucas came to me as a life-coaching client through my husband, Ken, whom he'd contacted first. In his introductory letter to Ken, he wrote, "I've followed you online for years, and followed your workout advice with enthusiasm and hope. I wanted to reach out to you now because of how pessimistic I have become because of my condition. You are a soldier and a fitness specialist; so I'm going to ask you a very, very hard question, and I can't blame you if you don't answer: What on earth do I do?

"At 24, instead of trying to join the Army, I'm stuck with an arm that can't even reach my mouth, and have been told to take it easy until me and my deformed arm both die. People like you don't know the word quit; how can I be like you in this moment?"

Lucas didn't need to be like my husband. He needed to find where he fit into the world at this present moment, regardless of his physical condition. Although he didn't realize it yet, the better question would have been, "How can I love myself despite my limitation?"

In our first coaching session together, Lucas shared the story of how he developed his long-term depression and hopelessness. After learning the Army wouldn't take him, he'd gone to college, and then graduate school for mechanical engineering. By age 24, he was a highly successful think-tank expert. He created original products and systems for the military as a contractor, and worked as an advisor to other engineers who also did product design for the military. He was like a young, real-life version of Marvel Comics' Tony Stark, the character who created the "Iron Man" suit.

But far from feeling like a superhero, Lucas remained focused on what he couldn't do. He devalued his accomplishments. His identity was built on his perceived deficits and a lack of self-worth. He was very unhappy.

To exemplify how he felt, he told me a story. One day, he was having lunch with a couple of friends who had joined the military right out of high school. One became a scout sniper in Iraq, and the other had been a Marine in Afghanistan.

Having just returned from traveling, Lucas joined the two friends in a café for a visit. They discussed the sightseeing Lucas had done and then talked about how their lives had taken different paths.

"How old are you, Lucas?" the Iraq veteran asked.

"21," Lucas replied.

"When I was 21, I was stepping off a plane into f—ing Baghdad," his friend responded. "More power to you, Lucas."

The comment felt like a direct attack. Although it may not have been intended that way, it reinforced Lucas' already diminished sense of personal value and lowered it even further. His physical disability had kept him from serving in that capacity, and this statement shamed him to the core.

When anyone made statements like this to him, comments that aligned with his poor self-image, it reinforced that image. He was caught in a cycle that kept him from believing that he mattered. If he couldn't belong to the group that would fill him with pride and significance—the military—then, he felt, he did not belong anywhere.

To move forward, Lucas would need to recognize and honor his strengths and talents. He was focused on lack of worth, when what he needed was to feel loved, appreciated and a sense of connectedness.

I began explaining the Belief Expectation Cycle to him.[1] Understanding it would be central to recognizing his self-limiting patterns.

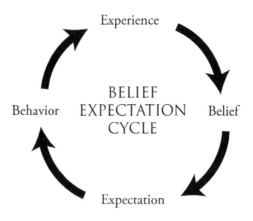

Experience

BELIEF
Behavior EXPECTATION Belief
CYCLE

Expectation

© Restoring The Foundations

"I think you're hitting very close though to one of my issues," Lucas told me, "which is the issue of worthiness. How do you know whether you are?"

"If I lined up 100 people," I told him, "nearly all of them, at some point in their lives, would have experienced feelings of unworthiness. However, when it becomes a cycle that impacts our behavior, and our responses to others and to the world, we need to see it for what it is so we can change it."

Revisiting the negative comments that had held Lucas back, I asked, "If we continued this conversation from the perspective of you as the coach, what do you think you'd hear as the overarching theme?"

"That I'm not good enough," he said. "And I guess, from a more sympathetic eye, helplessness."

Helplessness comes from feelings of unworthiness, and it was keeping Lucas stuck and feeling like an outsider. The underlying belief of unworthiness is, "There is something lacking in me. I'm not good enough." When we have this scarcity mindset, we feel like our contributions will never turn out well and that we won't matter enough to leave a lasting legacy.

The story Lucas told himself was one built on perceived inadequacies. He was focused on what he couldn't do instead of who he was and where he was headed. It was a dead-end thinking pattern, and it kept him from embracing his actual successes. He lost the race before he started it.

Although it took multiple sessions, Lucas began to see how the Belief Expectation Cycle was running his life. Up to this point, he'd believed he could never measure up in society. But once he recognized the cycle, he realized that by breaking it, he could reset his perspective and begin from a place of abundance—not lack. He needed to internalize the possibility that he could do great things despite his limitations.

SURVIVAL MODE

When we focus on what we lack, we live in survival mode, where it's hard to build hope for the future. Emotional poverty, otherwise known as a scarcity mindset, is a dream-killer. It makes us believe we've missed our opportunity—that our past is more relevant than our future. Even if we continually strive toward excellence, we feel like we'll never achieve it.

In this mode, we become isolated. We don't want people to see our emotional wounds. It feels easier to put up a veneer of perfection than to connect with others. So we remain feeling small, which drowns the seeds of joy. We think dysfunctional thoughts, because we don't realize we have the option to build positive emotions the same way we built the negative ones—one thought, one action at a time.

REJECT REJECTION

I once heard an African minister named Surprise (pronounced "Sue-pray-za") say, "Reject rejection."

In order to fill our emotional bank accounts, to find the courage to connect with others and pursue opportunities that require risk, we have to reject the idea that we're rejected by others. We need to dismiss our perceived flaws and see ourselves as likeable. This is when we can begin to believe we are enough.

It doesn't mean we become perfect. No one is. It's simply a conscious choice to take the focus off of our imperfections and treat ourselves with more kindness.

Like I told Lucas, and the boys at C.A.M.P., operating from a scarcity mindset is a choice. It's the result of a negative personal story we've told ourselves due to original negative experiences.

Our future is built upon the internal culture we create. The idea that we can't make a difference, that we'd be better off dead, that we should give up, needs to be lovingly challenged. We need to reject these thoughts and replace them with new ones.

If we don't reject the negativity, it will continue to rob us of peace and joy. The toxic thoughts must be seen for what they are and then released. They strangle the melody of our soul. We must believe we have something of value to offer. We have to be willing to show up and be all-in, despite nagging self-doubt.

Having faith in ourselves and in our future is a present-tense decision. It means we choose to take steps out of isolation and into a meaningful life. It means we rebuild our story based on a sense of value and the belief that we can make a difference. It means we begin to believe in ourselves.

COMMUNICATION WAS CENTRAL TO SURVIVAL

The late Senator John McCain was a fighter pilot in Vietnam who was shot down in Hanoi by a Vietnamese missile "the size of a telephone pole" on October 26, 1967.[2] He was on his 23rd mission. When he ejected from his Skyhawk bomber jet, the blast forced him into the side of the plane, knocking him unconscious and breaking both arms and his right leg. He landed in the water of the Trúc Bach Lake, known to Americans as the Western Lake, and was subsequently captured.[4]

When McCain was pulled from the water, despite his condition, he was spit on, hit, and stabbed by the Northern Vietnamese fighters. He was stripped down to his underwear and laid on a stretcher. For the next few days he fell in and out of consciousness.[4]

McCain was moved to Hòa Lò prison, known to the inmates as the "Hanoi Hilton." He was held captive for five-and-a-half years, spending more than two of them in solitary confinement. In an attempt to get him to release information, his captors tortured him with sleep deprivation, starvation, and beatings that left him with broken bones and cracked teeth. The miserable living conditions caused boils and dysentery.[2]

A few months after his arrival back in the United States, in the May 1973 issue of the U.S. News & World Report, McCain discussed the details of his captivity, and how he stayed alive and sane.[2] He received patience through prayer, stability by safeguarding his thoughts, and companionship by communicating with other captives. As he was able, he also added exercise to his daily routine. His biggest fight, he wrote, was with fear.

"Communication with your fellow prisoners was of the utmost value—the difference between being able to resist and not being able to resist," said McCain, referring to rough treatment and reprisals against him.[2] Although communication with inmates was sporadic while he was in solitary confinement, he continued to initiate contact. He would tap out messages on the wall using the alphabet—one tap for "a," two for "b," and so on. He would speak using a cup pressed to a wall, or by flashing code—sometimes to his own detriment.[2] It was his commitment to his fellow prisoners that kept his fight to stay alive burning inside of him.

Lt. Col. Orson Swindle, USMC Ret., one of McCain's fellow prisoners, recounted their first conversation, which was tapped out on the wall using code. McCain allegedly told an off-color joke. "We had been through so much that was terrifying and painful," Swindle continued, "we talked about everything we had ever done, remembered, thought of, hoped for. It was just an amazing friendship; he was a fascinating guy... We told stories about our kids and everything. Every movie we'd ever seen, every book we'd ever read." According to Swindle, during the last year of captivity, they even adlibbed the play "A Christmas Carol." McCain played Scrooge. Swindle added, "of course."[3] The bonds they formed during those years lasted a lifetime.

Following his release, McCain stayed in the Navy for approximately seven more years. After failing his physical, McCain retired from the military. He decided to focus on the future, what was still possible, and not his physical limitations, which prevented him from qualifying to continue in the only career he'd ever known. Within two years of his retirement, he ran for a seat in the House of Representatives, beginning his 45-year tenure in various public offices.

THE WAY FORWARD IS IN TELLING OUR STORY

There is a reason that connectedness sustained McCain. There's power in revealing our weaknesses, fears, hopes and dreams. It helps us understand that while our circumstances may be unique, our feelings aren't.

We need to reach out and share our stories with others. We can talk with a friend over coffee—one who has earned the right to hear our story by having been vulnerable with us, too. Or we might begin with therapy or a support group. Hearing others talk about their shame and imperfections helps normalize ours. Being around empathetic people allows us to be seen, heard and accepted. And it helps us turn the spotlight away from what we can't readily change and instead shines a healing light into our souls.

Abby Wambach, U.S. Soccer Olympic Gold Medalist and

best-selling author, illustrates strength through a strong support system in her book, *Wolfpack*. She writes, "Life is harder as a lone wolf. We all need a Pack."[5] Healthy connections make us stronger. She goes on to say, "In the end, owning and unleashing all your power isn't just about you… The Wolfpack's collective power begins by unleashing the power of each individual Wolf." When we stop focusing on our weaknesses, we begin to move into our potential. By doing so, we give others permission to do the same. Other people in our "Wolfpack" make up for our shortcomings. Connection is lifeblood.

> We all have aspects of our lives we'd like to change. Some are within our power, and some aren't. It's time to realign our vision and focus on what we're capable of doing instead of what we can't control.

When we've been isolated for a very long time, connection can feel scary. But over time, sharing our story with others becomes more natural, and we begin to see that our lives are part of a bigger story. We are valuable, lovable, and imperfectly perfect. Our scars and "flaws" are part of who we are. We all have them.

So, how do we lose the scarcity mindset? We reject rejection. We aren't the only one—we all have flaws, weaknesses, and shortcomings. We will realize it when we risk coming out of isolation. There is healing if we will step into the power of community.

It's time to tell the story that wounded our souls.

Abundant possibility awaits.

HERE'S WHAT I WOULD SAY TO TREVOR AND TO YOU

We all have aspects of our lives we'd like to change. Some are within our power, and some aren't. It's time to realign our vision and focus on what we're capable of doing instead of what we can't control.

When the scarcity mindset takes over, try using these questions for reflection:

1. How have you been stuck in scarcity thinking? How has this mindset been holding you back?

2. With what group would you like to connect (i.e. church, a 12-step program, etc.)?

3. If you believed you had the power to create change in your life right now, what is one new action you might take?

Choose to see what's right for you. Focus not on where you fall short, but on what you do well and where you'd like to make a difference. Choose connection. There is hope for your situation.

· · · · · · · · · · · · · · · · · · · ·

References

1. Kylstra, C., & Kylstra, B. (n.d.). [Belief Expectation Cycle, Restoring the Foundations Nonprofit Ministry].

2. McCain, J. (2008, January 28). John McCain, Prisoner of War: A First-Person Account. Retrieved July 1, 2019, from https://www.usnews.com/news/articles/2008/01/28/john-mccain-prisoner-of-war-a-first-person-account

3. Melton, M. (2018, September 1). Former POWs Remember John McCain in Vietnam. Retrieved July 1, 2019, from https://www.voanews.com/a/former-pows-remember-john-mccain-in-vietnam/4553641.html

4. The Story of John Sidney McCain III. (n.d.). Retrieved July 1, 2019, from https://www.johnmccain.com/story/

5. Wambach, A. (2019). Wolfpack: How To Come Together, Unleash Our Power, and Change the Game. New York: Celadon Books.

CHAPTER THREE

STRATEGY #3:
CHANGE THE STORY

―――――

"Beliefs have the power to create and the power to destroy. Human beings have the awesome ability to take any experience of their lives and create a meaning that disempowers them or one that can literally save their lives."

—Tony Robbins

IN OUR FIRST session together, Stephen told his story.

"My job sucks," he said. "I don't own my own house. I don't feel significant."

After hundreds of hours studying, three advanced degrees, and graduating top ten in his class, he felt like a failure because he wasn't working in his chosen career field.

But this wasn't always the case. Twenty years earlier, just out of college, he had his dream job—a high-profile position in advertising. "I worked on the 28th floor of a high-rise in the downtown business section," he told me. "It was a high-pressure job. You had to maintain peak performance to survive." It was a job he loved, and one he felt defined him. The work was exciting and made him feel powerful.

But over time, the pressure became a problem. The stress it caused triggered a dangerous autoimmune response. A visit to the doctor revealed that his condition was life-threatening. He was forced to make the hardest decision of his life: Quit the job or die.

He left the job to seek treatment and ended up moving back in with his parents until he recovered. In the intense self-criticism that followed, he began backing away from relationships and new opportunities. Now, 20 years later, he was still telling himself that he was a professional failure. He was focused on who he hadn't become, instead of what he had accomplished in life so far.

To Stephen, a sense of significance seemed out of reach, because it was tied to an inflexible vision of success he could no longer achieve. Leaving the job and moving back in with his parents felt like defeat. The suit-wearing executive who worked in a tall, down-town building was his image of success, and he wasn't living up to it. Instead of the high-status job and handsome salary, he had to take a local job to help pay the bills. It was the responsible thing to do, but it directly impacted his self-esteem.

He believed he was a failure and would never be good enough.

"It broke my spirit and made me fear being ambitious," he said. "I lost confidence."

Returning to the root of the problem, I said, "Leaving the job saved your life." Although it felt like his hand had been forced, I said, quitting had been his choice. This was a new perspective for him. He'd never thought of that decision as a conscious choice or seen it as a positive move.

But hearing his story from my objective point of view, one untainted by judgment about his success and failure, gradually helped him see that there were still opportunities for him to succeed.

Over the course of our sessions, his old story and feelings about the outcome began to shift. He was able to reclaim a sense of dignity.

After working with me for a while, Stephen expressed, "I've been revisiting the story I tell myself about what happened to me while working in advertising, and I'm not at the mercy of those negative thoughts any more." Instead of seeing quitting as failure, he now saw it as a wake-up call—because the pressure was literally killing him. He actually did something positive by quitting: He chose life.

When our definition of success, achievement, and significance are tied to goals we feel powerless to achieve, our emotions help reinforce that false narrative. It's hard to envision what we don't believe.

THE POWERLESS STORY

During one of his large conferences, best-selling author and business coach Tony Robbins shared an anecdote to show how people can talk themselves out of seeing what's right in front of them.[3]

He described a family having dinner at their dining room table. The mom turned to her young son and asked him to go get the salt from the kitchen. Not wanting to do the task, the boy sighed loudly as he stomped off. "I don't know where the salt is," he called, staring blankly at the spices. "Moooooooom, come help me!"

Not leaving her seat, mom responded, "It's in the cabinet to the left of the microwave."

As his frustration grew, the directions were lost on the boy. "I can't find it!" he repeated. "It's not here!"

Mom quietly walked into the kitchen and stood behind her aggravated child. Much to his surprise, she pulled the salt (which was at eye level in front of him) off the shelf.

Many of us have experienced this story for ourselves. When the boy said he couldn't find the salt, he effectively told his brain it wasn't there. It was as though he made an agreement with himself to not see it, even though it was sitting in front of his face. His capacity to see became congruent with what he believed. His words became a self-fulfilling prophecy. Although the salt could have been easily found, his beliefs placed a limitation on his ability.

Our negative beliefs about our future will place the same limitation on our ability to see success.

THE STORIES WE TELL OURSELVES

The way we think about and tell our stories either motivates us or limits us. When we believe we can't be successful, we prevent ourselves from recognizing our achievements.

At some level, each of us has such a story. When something doesn't meet our expectations, we equate that to failure. When a situation with a family member, friend or acquaintance goes badly, we may think of ourselves as unlovable or unworthy. We personalize the pain. It feeds our perceived lack of self-worth. Additional negative stories continue to feed this lie. The pain reinforces the feeling of isolation leading to an inability to create positive emotion.
To restore our power, we have to examine the story from a different perspective. We need to see ourselves in the driver's seat—in control of our future.

We must become the hero in our story.

THE WAY FORWARD

We change our behavior a little at a time by recreating our narrative. We take small, daily actions that snowball into bigger events. We reach out to friends and join groups to build meaningful connections.

Even though we can't always see how things will work out, we press forward with our best efforts. And those small steps and daily actions become the stepping-stones to higher ground.

It's not that we don't have losses. We do. In fact, we may be in the middle of a huge mess. The negative narrative may resurface. But we don't allow ourselves to stay stuck in it. We reach out for help, for a fresh perspective. We cultivate a deep sense of knowing that, if we don't give up, the small seeds we plant daily will eventually yield a harvest. We change the story.

The shift starts not with our circumstances, but with our beliefs.

To restore our power, we have to examine the story from a different perspective. We need to see ourselves in the driver's seat—in control of our future.

We must become the hero in our story.

SELF-FULFILLING PROPHECY

We often tell ourselves things that aren't true. We connect our destiny and sense of worthiness to a life we think we'll acquire at some point—after we check specific boxes on our list. As long as those boxes remain unchecked, we can't find fulfillment in the present. We don't enjoy the journey. Our inner critic says, "See I told you so—your dreams are impossible."

We feed the negative narrative by repeatedly revisiting the image of the person we believed we should have become, how we didn't achieve it, and how we may never achieve it. We isolate ourselves, quit setting goals, and stop the flow of meaningful connection. Our proverbial heartbeat grows dull.

We have to re-evaluate our old stories. To do this, we can use the Belief Expectation Cycle in a five-step process of questions and reflections.[1]

THE FIVE-STEP PROCESS

Step One: Experience
What was the activating event? What happened? This is the

experience that started the snowball effect. This is where our story became rooted in a sense of unworthiness. It could have been something as simple as a negative comment or more traumatic such as a major life incident, or an accident. To someone else, it may not have appeared significant. But to us, it was, and that's what counts.

Step Two: Value Statement
Following the activating event, what was our internal value statement about our identity? At its core, it's usually something about feeling unworthy, unloved, or inadequate.

Step Three: Belief
What belief did we build around our perceived lack of worth? Did we develop a vision that equated value with a specific achievement? When we didn't attain that goal, what did we begin to believe about ourselves?

For me, it was not being in the right industry, in a nine-to-five job. That was my early adulthood picture of success. And because I didn't have it, I continually felt like a failure. The belief was that I somehow missed my destiny. So happiness felt out of reach for me.

Feelings of success breed success. Feelings of failure keep us feeling like failures.

Step Four: Response
How do we respond to our feelings? Do we wake up each day buying into our old story, operating under our old assumptions, and reconnecting with that feeling of hopelessness?

Step Five: Behavior
What kind of actions do we engage in if this feeling persists? It's in this step where we repeat behavior patterns that cause low self-worth and rob us of a sense of belonging. Because we lack an innate sense of worthiness, we feel we need to protect ourselves, and may unintentionally hide and keep people at arms' length.

BRAIN RESEARCH

According to brain researcher Dr. Caroline Leaf, repeating positive thoughts is like water and sunshine to a tree.[2] They grow and become stronger. Our thoughts release chemicals, and the chemicals create emotions that reflect those thoughts. If the emotions are negative, the chemicals produced can create stress and sickness. However, the brain can form new pathways if we intentionally build a new way of thinking. This is the precursor for new actions.

To change our circumstances, we have to begin with different thoughts. We have to challenge our false story of hopelessness, where we're the victim, or too far down the wrong path to recover. Some circumstances are beyond our control. But many times, we make poor choices because we don't believe we have the power to create our future.

Going back to Tony Robbins' example of the boy who couldn't see the salt, we can believe our old story to the point where we cripple our ability to see any other ending. It can make us feel small and keep us from connecting with others.

We can dredge up the same anger, the same shock, the same feelings of unworthiness we've always had, or we can change our mental image. Either way, our story will influence our nervous system. Moving forward begins with telling that story then, reframing the story and recasting ourselves as the hero—not the downtrodden victim, or worse, the villain. We remind ourselves about our victories—no matter how small they may seem —and what we've done well. We focus on these new stories to replace the old ones.

When we change the way we see our story, we develop the ability to design our future. We realize that good things are possible, that we can connect with others, and that we can have a sense of purpose. Then we begin with a few actionable next steps, in the form of goals.

TIME BRINGS PERSPECTIVE

What if each of us could see that by taking those next steps, our lives would one day make sense? That our purpose would emerge? What if we could find assurance here and now, in this waiting period, that the pieces of our life will eventually fit together?

Good things take time to unfold. It can take many years for certain events to make sense, and in some cases, we may never know why they happened. But if we choose to keep moving forward, we may discover how they make sense in the context of our greater purpose.

Our story can render us powerless or motivate us to keep moving toward hope. There is always a choice. You must be the hero in your own story—even if you can't see how it will work out.

Like the doctor said to the patient whose heart wouldn't start after surgery: It's time to wake back up. Tell your heart to beat again.

HERE'S WHAT I WOULD SAY TO TREVOR AND TO YOU

When we continue to experience pain, isolation, anxiety, and stress, we have to look at the root of the problem. It's important to notice the story you've been telling yourself. It matters because the negative feelings it produces can keep you from moving toward your biggest aspirations.

Are you telling yourself, "Things will never change?" If your story renders you powerless, anxious, or isolated, it's time to change those habitual thoughts and words.

Use these questions for reflection:

1. What story have you been telling yourself? How does that story impact your feelings of self-worth?

2. What might be a positive, new perspective on your old situation?

3. How can you tell the old story in a way that is life-affirming? How might this new version of your story empower you to make a change in your life?

Steve Jobs, founder of Apple once said, "Those who are crazy enough to think they can change the world usually do." Are you telling yourself you can change the world? If you choose to internalize that idea, you can be a world-changer.

The events in your old story may be true. However, your past does not own your future. Begin to tell yourself a new story—one that empowers you.

. . . .

References

1. Kylstra, C., & Kylstra, B. (n.d.). [Belief Expectation Cycle, Restoring the Foundations Nonprofit Ministry].

2. Leaf, Caroline (2009) Who Switched Off My Brain? Controlling Toxic Thoughts and Emotions. Published by Inprov, Ltd. pp. 19-20.

3. Robbins, T., Pesha, M., & Madanes, C. (2013, July 01). "Salt Story", Robbins Madanes Training. Lecture. Retrieved from https://rmtcenter.com/.

SECOND LIFE LESSON: LEARN TO TOUGH OUT THE TENSION

I LOVE THE movie *Indiana Jones and the Last Crusade*. One epic scene in particular stands the test of time as an illustration of courage in moving forward despite fear and uncertainty, and despite the story that plays in our minds.

In the movie[2], Indiana (Indy) Jones and his father, Henry Jones Sr., embark on a treasure hunt for the Holy Grail. When the enemy wounds Henry, Indy must find the cup that will save his father's life.[1] Along the journey, he encounters physical challenges that will either bring him closer to the Holy Grail or—with any misstep—kill him.

Following the path on his hand-drawn map, Indy emerges from a cave to find that the trail he's on ends abruptly. He sees nothing but an enormous, black, seemingly bottomless chasm in front of him. He double-checks his map to make sure this is the correct route. It is.

Indy is in a seemingly no-win situation. Standing in place means losing his father. But taking the next step, with no visible bridge across the chasm, appears to be a free-fall to his own certain death.

"It's impossible," he says to himself. "Nobody can jump this."

His chest heaves with fear as he tries to think of any other way. Realizing there's none, he says, "It's a leap of faith."

Thinking this might be his final act of courage, Indy puts his hand over his heart, and with beads of sweat running down his dirty face, he does the unthinkable. He raises his left leg high in the air and slowly steps forward.

To his amazement, his foot lands on solid ground—an invisible bridge made of stone. He was unable to see it because it blended into the lines of the surrounding cliffs and depended on his faith to step out of his comfort zone into the abyss.

As he moves forward, one step after another, the bridge never becomes visible to Indy. It can only be seen from a side view—the perspective he doesn't have. He must continue crossing it without ever seeing it.

Many times, the path between where we are and where we want to be is obscured. We can't see it because we don't have the perspective. The way forward can feel very uncertain—like a step into the unknown. We know our dreams are on the other side, but we can't see how to get there. When we decide to take that step, it has to be with the belief that getting there *is* possible.

Instead of focusing on who we aren't, we have to focus on who we *are*. We can't make progress by waiting for certainty to come. The ability to attain our goal is based on what we tell ourselves today.

When we set out into the unknown, it may be a while before our surroundings look any different. But little by little, we're changing on the inside. We may feel uncomfortable in our own skin while we keep an unwanted job a while longer, stay in a floundering relationship, be kind to relatives or coworkers who haven't been kind to us, chip away at an unrelenting debt load, continue to treat an illness, or re-learn to connect with people after a painful past.

Real change requires us to do something that feels unfamiliar. We have to leave the safety and security of what's familiar, and step into the unknown.

The way out of pain, isolation, and suffering is rarely glamorous. It can feel gut-wrenching—like eating adrenaline for lunch or stepping off a cliff to our death. What we don't realize, until we're farther down the path, is that the real death is in not moving forward.

We need hope and courage to do this. We may have to cross more than one bridge. Success isn't guaranteed. But we can count on this: We'll never get where we hope to go if we stay where we are. Loving relationships, fulfilling careers, and promising futures await us on the other side.

The next few chapters show us how to interrupt the cycle of negative emotions and begin building personal resilience. They transition us from the broad overview we've already explored to a more granular look at these concepts and how to implement them on a day-to-day basis.

Chapter Four presents an alternative point of view, opening us up to new solutions to old problems. In chapter Five, we continue learning to recognize and eliminate dead-end thinking patterns that dissolve hope and personal value. In chapter Six, we revisit the topic of changing the inner dialogue.

· · · · · · · · · · · · · · · · · · · ·

References

1. Indiana Jones and the Last Crusade (1989). (n.d.). Retrieved November 28, 2017, from http://www.imdb.com/title/tt0097576/

2. Indiana Jones and the Last Crusade. (2010, September 07). Retrieved November 28, 2017, from https://www.youtube.com/watch?v=xFntFdEGgws

STRATEGY #4
FIND THE THIRD SOLUTION

*"The law of attraction states that whatever you focus
on, think about, read about, and talk about intensely,
you're going to attract more of into your life."*

—Jack Canfield

"ON A COUPLE of occasions, I'd sit in my car after work
and just cry, feeling fed up with my job and wishing there
was something better. I'd also feel overwhelmed."

Jacob, one of my coaching clients, was a business analyst by day
and a fitness coach by night. He'd recently realized he no longer
wanted the day job; he wanted to be a full-time trainer. But he was
supporting his wife and two young children, and felt like he couldn't
leave for the financial uncertainty of an entrepreneurial life. Being
an analyst didn't tap into his creativity or desire to help people. But
the life of a fitness coach seemed too risky financially, because clients
can be unreliable.

He saw only two courses of action—keep his job, or quit and

risk financial ruin. Both seemed unacceptable. He felt stuck. The belief that he was powerless to change his circumstances left him depressed, anxious, and angry, masking any sense of peace, joy, or self-worth.

Jacob *was* stuck, but not in the way he thought. He was trapped in either/or thinking. Either remain at the day job *or* follow his dream. From his point of view, those were the only two scenarios.

But what if there was another option—a third solution? What if we could step outside of our traditional thought processes and see another possibility?

A breakthrough past the anxiety requires us to dream creatively about our future. Because our dreams rarely take a direct, straight-line route, point A to point B, the third solution is about taking baby steps forward, and then relaxing into the meandering, character-shaping process that achieving our dream takes. We can't follow dreams that we can't first imagine.

To help Jacob consider a third solution, I asked him if it was possible to use his talents in his day job. Instead of quitting, could he find ways to express his creativity and help others at the office? Instead of feeling like a prisoner of his circumstances, could he gain a sense of control in his existing situation?

He felt like it was a possibility. He considered the idea of blooming where he was planted. He wasn't in his dream job, but he could try to make the most of his situation. He began by taking on small side roles at work, as a coach. He wrote wellness articles for the company's e-newspaper and held fitness classes at company events. He assumed a leadership and mentoring position in his current position. And at night, and on weekends, he studied for certifications that would enhance his coaching practice.

Gradually, he began to feel more fulfilled. Although his actual job hadn't changed appreciably, his attitude had. Interestingly, the pieces of his life fell into place a year later. Unexpectedly laid off from his job, he was able to transition into being a full-time coach, thanks to the coaching skills he'd developed at work and in his spare time.

THE THIRD SOLUTION

The third solution is a part of the messy middle. It's the point after we've creatively dreamed about possibilities, goals, accomplishments, careers, trips, and families, when it seems like life may never align with that big vision.

The paradox of the third solution is that we can only recognize it if we've started dreaming about something we're not yet chasing. It's the "thing" we can't seem to shake from our mind. It's a dream, desire, wish, or a bucket list item. If it's not a specific job, it could be a sense of stability when everything feels unstable. It may be a story we want to publish—or a family we want to start, when we haven't even started dating. Perhaps it's more than one thing.

The third solution is the point where reality looks like the opposite of our dream. But it's also when our roots grow deep and strong. This is where we change from the inside out. If we can become mindful that, for a while, our circumstances won't match the richness and fullness of our vision of the future, we can be flexible about the present even when that future seems impossible.

BABY STEPS

The path to a dream is often fraught with life's lumps.

A young writer named Joanne was in need of a fresh start after her mother passed. Although she carried a fanciful story in her heart, she had barely begun writing her novel before she moved from her home in the U.K. to Northern Portugal to teach English. She fell in love with a man, got pregnant and moved in with him. The couple soon married and had a baby girl. However, they divorced when their daughter was only 13 months old.

Devastated and destitute, Joanne moved back to the U.K. with her daughter and, for a while, survived on government assistance. Every day, she went to cafés and worked on the novel she'd started before her mother's passing, with her daughter asleep at her side.

She had endured poverty, being a single parent, and—in her own words—"loads" of rejection letters from book publishers. But in 1997, seven years after she'd started writing, Bloomsbury Publishing decided to take a chance on her novel, *Harry Potter and the Philosopher's Stone,* written under her pen name, J.K. Rowling.[2]

Breakthrough looks a lot like perseverance in the dark times, from a path that often seems bleak and full of unexpected twists and turns. For Rowling, it was a drive to tell a story and publish it. For others it might not be as clear. For all of us, it begins with a dream in mind.

FLEXIBLE THINKING

The saying "think outside the box" has become a bit of a cliché, but it applies to the third solution. It's a resilient approach to dealing with the uncharted path toward our deepest desires. It means setting aside our current assumptions—*I'm doomed to hate my day job; but if I leave I'll fail financially*—and finding new possibilities. It's blooming where we're planted by taking the smallest steps toward our goals, despite how insignificant those steps feel.

So what hinders flexible thinking? Why isn't it easy or automatic? Why doesn't it come naturally?

LIMITLESS POWER

When we're not thinking flexibly and creatively, there are many possible reasons. Our situation might look like the complete opposite of what we pictured for ourselves. A major event might have derailed us midstride. We may feel like we're too old.

One of the most common underlying reasons is a sense of

disempowerment. We simply stopped believing we have the ability to achieve our big dreams.

I watched this problem play out during Jack Canfield's keynote speech for several thousand fitness professionals at the 2016 IDEA World Fitness Convention[1]. Canfield is the author of the best-selling book *Chicken Soup for the Soul* and the *Chicken Soup* series that came after. His speech was entitled *The Success Principles: How to Get From Where You Are to Where You Want to Be*.

He discussed how our negative beliefs keep us limited. To offer a visual example, he invited a woman to the stage who was a well-regarded fitness presenter and life coach. Canfield was about to show the audience the physical connection between disempowering thoughts and reduced muscle strength.

In the exercise, he had her lift her left arm sideways, parallel with the floor, and then told her to resist when he tried to push her arm down. She was strong, so she withstood quite a bit of pressure before he succeeded.

Then he asked her to think about taking a six-month vacation from work.

"Could you take the time off?" he prodded. Her arm was still extended.

"No," she responded.

This time, he pushed her arm down with ease. It was an impressive visual demonstration of how our beliefs affect our power.

I had to love her honesty. It sounded like a great idea, but she did not believe she could afford this type of luxury. In a later, private conversation with her, I found out the hidden truth. Her full-time job was stifling her—her real desire was to pursue her entrepreneurial dreams.

Canfield had presented this accomplished woman with an either/or scenario. Either she could take the time off or she couldn't. She wanted to, but because she felt she couldn't, she became disempowered. Her strength disappeared. Her belief that the statement was true rendered her (and her arm) powerless.

This is a metaphor for life. When we doubt that we can achieve our dreams, we lose strength.

So how can we reclaim our power? By finding peace in the process of moving toward the life we desire, we begin to replace disempowering fears with empowering thoughts.

Christian speaker Bill Johnson once said to a large audience, "How many of you have become so anxious over something, it kept you up at night? You had that thing going through your brain all night long and you couldn't sleep?"[3] Hands across the auditorium went up. "Alright. We know that we know how to meditate." The audience erupted into laughter. "So now we just have to change the subject matter." He explained that we can change our recurring thought by meditating on the Bible. His "camping spot"—his go-to Bible verses—was found in Joshua 1, and was a resource he once used to help him through a health crisis. The full passage, he said, brought him "rest and refreshing."

Whatever resource we choose for inspiration, we can replace fear-based thoughts with life-giving ideas. Instead of allowing ourselves to fixate on concepts we feel powerless to control, we can redirect our thoughts and even choose to say the new ones out loud. Tony Robbins calls these powerful and purposeful sayings "incantations." Other people call them affirmations. It's when we deliberately think about or verbalize positive sayings—something of our choosing, rather than something we're worried about.

THE CLOSED LOOP

When we believe we're at the end of a road or out of options, we may begin to feel despair. We focus on what's not possible instead of what is. This mindset can become normal for us—just "how we think." And in the process, our self-worth becomes directly tied to circumstances we feel powerless to change.

Such a thought pattern creates a closed loop. We don't act

because we feel disempowered. Negative emotion results from inaction. Whatever courage we once had dissolves. We stay stuck on the ledge, unable to take the necessary step—the leap of faith. Unless we become willing to try, to take a baby step forward, the cycle will continue.

Finding a solution to our current dilemma requires choosing new words and thoughts that can restore hope and a sense of power. It also means taking the next small step forward, even if our circumstances still look dismal. This is how we erase the period at the end of the sentence that used to define our past, and add an "and" or a "but" to move toward a brighter future.

When we doubt that we can achieve our dreams, we lose strength. So how can we reclaim our power? By finding peace in the process of moving toward the life we desire, we begin to replace disempowering fears with empowering thoughts.

Jacob worked on developing his skill set in a job that once brought him to tears. Rowling wrote her book slowly, over time, as a single mom living on government assistance. In the midst of Rowling's challenging circumstances, she had no way of knowing she would become an iconic, best-selling author. Jacob, too, had no way of knowing how things would turn out.

So, how do we escape the closed loop?

SMALL STEPS

When we first set out to try, we can't see the whole picture. We may only see a couple of steps ahead. And those steps may look small, which can make the goal seem unattainable. So we struggle to see the value in taking them. They may even seem arduous—like putting one foot in front of the other on a winding path to nowhere.

But we need to change that perspective. Small steps are the key to major transformation. Sometimes they're not well defined.

We may begin in one direction, and then turn and take a different path. For instance, we may take a job that doesn't work out and find ourselves having to begin again in a new job. Or, like Rowling, we may have to learn to take small steps forward, despite how we feel and our present circumstances, while we continue to plan, set goals, and dream about the future.

Remember how Indiana Jones had to cross the invisible bridge to find the Holy Grail? For him, stepping forward felt like plunging toward death. It can feel that way to us, too, especially if past risks we've taken turned out badly. We can't know how good the outcome will be until we have the perspective of overcoming our challenge.

HERE'S WHAT I WOULD SAY TO TREVOR AND TO YOU

If someone who knew your future told you that you'd do many wonderful things with your life, would you believe it? Or would you say, "There's no way that could happen. That's too big, costs too much money, I don't have the right connections."

Moving toward your greatest destiny requires a level of comfort in the uncomfortable. There may not be a direct route. You may have to look past the obvious choices for a third solution.

Like Indiana Jones, you can't look at things for what they are. You have to imagine them for what they could be, and then take baby steps toward that vision.

This doesn't mean negative thoughts won't try to derail you. They might. But it means you keep moving forward in a positive, new direction anyway. There's an invisible bridge that separates you from your promise. Getting across the bridge requires facing your fears.

Very often, the key to success lies in the connections we haven't yet made. If we take even the first few steps, we'll be prepared when the opportunity, the right connections, finally come along.

Questions for reflection:

1. How would you benefit if you opened yourself up to a third solution—a new perspective on this problem? What might that third option entail?

2. How would it change your life if you moved toward this new option?

3. What small steps do you need to take now to set yourself up for success in that area?

Heading toward the less obvious choice can make you feel vulnerable. Being vulnerable exposes you to pain. But that pain won't last. Don't make long-term decisions based on temporary pain. Remember that the presence of pain is not an indicator of your level of worthiness or future accomplishments and is often part of the growing and maturing process.

You have a song to be played. Your melody is a gift for someone else within your sphere of influence. Stay heartened. Keep playing.

. . . .

References

1. Canfield, J. (2016, July 14). The Success Principles: How to Get From Where You Are to Where You Want to Be. Speech presented at IDEA World 2016 in Los Angeles Convention Center, Los Angeles.

2. Gillett, R. (2015, May 18). From Welfare to One of the World's Wealthiest Women - the Incredible Rags-to-Riches Story of J.K. Rowling. Retrieved July 1, 2019, from https://www.businessinsider.com/the-rags-to-riches-story-of-jk-rowling-2015-5

3. Johnson, B. (Ed.). (2019, April 14). Meditate on Things Above - Sunday PM. Retrieved July 2, 2019, from https://www.bethel.tv/watch/7715

CHAPTER FIVE

STRATEGY #5: AVOID COUNTERPRODUCTIVE HABITS

===========

*"Edit your life frequently and ruthlessly.
It's your masterpiece after all."*

—Nathan W. Morris

IT WAS OUR fifth coaching session in two months. Lucas was the young man who had dreamed of joining Special Forces but was unable to enlist due to his shoulder disability. I was excited to learn how far he'd come since our last coaching session a week earlier. After reviewing his homework from the previous week, I asked, "What habits are you becoming aware of?"

"I'm realizing I put myself down frequently," responded Lucas. "I'm noticing a lot of self-doubt. I'm always comparing my childhood dreams to what I have today, and realizing how helpless that makes me feel. I get overwhelmed, and throw my hands up in the air, and say, 'To heck with it.'

"I'm afraid of ending up like my colleagues 37 years from now. They all seem like they're stagnating professionally; performing the same job they had when I first walked into the company seven years ago.

"Then I think, 'Is this my world for the next 37 years? Will I ever get to work on meaningful projects? Will I get a promotion? Should I go to another organization?' This is the only place I've ever worked, so there's a lot I don't know. Are the crazy things here the same everywhere? Do I want to try and relocate? Do I want to get another job in this region?"

Lucas told me that on his first date with his girlfriend, she'd asked him, "What is your dream job?" She had no idea it was a loaded question.

"Well, I will never have my dream job," he answered. "My dream job was to be a soldier. To go to dangerous places, do dangerous things, and save people."

Lucas and I discussed his being stuck in either/or scenarios. In his mind, he was either a hero or a bored engineer who didn't earn enough money for the kind of life he wanted to live. He believed his physical disability condemned him to a mundane life in which he couldn't accomplish anything.

He feared he would lose his girlfriend if he couldn't create a stable life for them—which he felt meant improving his income and buying a house that he currently couldn't afford.

But he was also afraid to make a change. "Do I want to abandon my engineering degree with the hope that I can pursue my dream somewhere else? Or, do I want to keep with the track I'm on, because I've already invested ten years of my life into it?"

His habit wasn't something he *did*, a perpetual way of thinking that crippled his sense of being able to make a contribution. His self-doubt was part of a vicious cycle.

While he didn't choose his disability, he did have control over his daily string of unanswerable questions that caused him to spiral into hopelessness. He gave himself no room to be powerful in his own story.

We get stuck by unintentionally recreating behavior that keeps us from growing. But by making a conscious decision to change this behavior, we make a shift toward change.

Counterproductive habits are unique to each individual. For some, it's asking either/or questions such as, "Either I achieve a certain goal or I am a failure." For many, it might be checking their phone instead of connecting with others. For some, it's something dangerous to their health, such as an addiction.

Habitual, debilitating thought and behavior patterns will persist until the cycle is intentionally broken.

To illustrate this point, I'll use what I call the Three Stage Behavior Change Model. The model I designed shows how we make and sustain change.

Stage One: Choices are associated with feelings about self-worth.

Stage Two: Choices are no longer associated with self-worth but remain steeped in self-limiting patterns.

Stage Three: Choices are based on personal value, and long-term habits are developed from the life-or-death principle.

Stage One

In the first stage, our choices and behavior are directly linked to our perception of our personal value. When we encounter an event that triggers negative emotions, we repeat old behavior patterns—which only reaffirms the negative feeling and continues the cycle. Lucas' counterproductive habit was questioning his options and believing he had only two.

Stage Two

In the second stage, we understand our fundamental feelings of unworthiness, but our self-limiting habits persist. We continue with behavior that holds us back. For example, Lucas may begin to change his perception of his self-worth, but he would need to purposefully curtail his negative thought pattern of counterproductive questions. Becoming aware of our old habits gives us the power to create new ones.

Stage Three

The third stage is where we want to be. At this stage, we recognize when we are slipping into self-limiting behavior and thinking, and replace these habits with something different. We have to make a conscious effort to produce a different response pattern while still facing the same problem or stimulus. It doesn't mean we don't have moments of self-doubt; it's that we choose to limit the thoughts and actions that keep us stuck in defeat and despair. At this stage, Lucas would be replacing his habit by using his creativity to imagine a new, prosperous future. Then he would make a list of goals that would help him achieve that vision.

BORROWING TROUBLE

After my husband and I moved out to the East Bay, I began a short-term employment contract with a company that worked with the military. The assignment had the potential to become long-term or even full time. For me, it was a dream job. Although it wasn't at a fashion company—my first choice—I finally had my desk in the marketing department. I was ecstatic! I felt like I belonged somewhere at last.

The trouble with it being a temporary position was that I felt like I had to prove my worth constantly. Because of that, I never really let my guard down. I tried to project an all-knowing, never-vulnerable, always-happy personality.

As my contract was coming to a close, I began to focus on whether or not it would be renewed. It was incessantly on my mind. Despite my best effort to put on a "show," I felt extremely negative and dejected. I had a hard time showing people my true self because I clung to a belief that the worst would happen. I wanted to be accepted but didn't really believe I would be. The more I tried to show my co-workers my value, the less it worked.

I was devastated the day the marketing director pulled me into a side office to let me know they were not renewing my contract. For me, it was a blow to my sense of identity and value. I needed to fit in. Moreover, this job had allowed me to believe in myself.

This instance was representative of a level-one thinking pattern. My interactions with people were based on fear and the perpetual feeling that I was not enough. The deeper problem wasn't about being accepted; it was that I needed to believe I was acceptable—and loved and valued—regardless of the job. I operated at a deficit until I decided to finally stop believing the worst.

For me, ending the negative cycle meant I had to give myself permission to believe in myself—to believe I was perfectly acceptable. It was only when I made a concerted effort to change that I did change. I had to dig in and be purposeful in my decision to end the negativity, to begin being vulnerable with others and to allow people to see my weaknesses and failures along with my successes and accomplishments.

Martha Beck, a sociologist and life coach often featured in O, The Oprah Magazine, describes how some people receive "secondary gains" from counterproductive habits—a benefit or advantage to hanging onto their problem.[1] Mine was a sense of personal safety. By seeking approval for my work performance, I kept people at arms' length emotionally, which meant avoiding the risk of being rejected as a person. I could only be rejected for my performance.

We might ask ourselves if our counterproductive habit or thought is rooted in an unconscious "benefit"—if we use it to mask a sense of fear or unworthiness. Because it's hard to know for sure, Beck suggests using the following question with a friend, coach, or therapist: "What rewards do you think I may be getting from my most frustrating problem?"

Habits will remain until the pain of keeping them outweighs the pain of changing. We will stay rooted in unworthiness, and counterproductive thinking and behavior, until we opt to replace those habits with life-affirming thoughts and behaviors. We will never truly find peace until we abandon our bad habits. Changing the channel in our minds is a choice.

Change happens when we decide to act from a place of worthiness and have faith in ourselves. Then, we begin to realize our future holds more for us than we thought—untapped purpose. We believe we are enough just the way we are. We become kinder and gentler to ourselves. We allow ourselves time to be known. We recognize our counterproductive behavior as a form of self-protection (more about that in chapters Eight and Nine). We develop the ability to envision a bright future, choose to believe we are lovable and valuable to others, and begin to allow people into our lives. When negative thoughts come creeping back to remind us of our deficiencies, we choose a thought or action that, rather than reinforce negativity, will bear fruit.

At different points in our lives, Lucas and I had the same underlying beliefs. For Lucas, his constant questioning kept him safe. But it also prevented him from thinking creatively about what he would like to attract into his life. His negative story blocked his ability to recognize opportunities or focus on a positive new direction.

We unintentionally prescribe the life we attract—safe, impenetrable, and disconnected.

COUNTERPRODUCTIVE HABITS

In the past, our counterproductive habits may have been a shield to protect us. But if they aren't moving us forward, they're keeping us stuck, isolated, and unhappy.

Below is a list of counterproductive habits that might prevent positive change from occurring. The list isn't comprehensive, but it's a place to start.

- Constantly believing we don't belong, are unworthy, or that we will be rejected.

- Believing the worst about ourselves.

- Obsessive worry.

- Focusing on the negative side of things.

- Creating an impenetrable veneer.

- Hiding from others when we feel vulnerable.

- Endless questions about how we'll fix our current situation.

- Using or doing something unhealthy to avoid emotional pain.

- Calling ourselves derogatory names.

- Telling ourselves that we deserve bad things.

- Telling ourselves anything negative, repeatedly.

- Doing the same things every day and hoping for a different result.

- Being caustic, unfriendly, or mean in order to self-protect.

- Rejecting ownership of the outcome.

PUTTING THE PROCESS INTO ACTION

Living in the tension means making new choices despite feeling small or hurt. It means being willing to step out of the safety that the secondary gain provides. I realized my own secondary gain from staying impenetrable meant that no one could reject my personality or my creativity. Changing meant being willing to be seen as my imperfect self.

What might happen if we allowed others past the armor, to see our quirky, creative, imaginative selves? What if we chose to hope for something, to step out in faith toward the thing we desire most? Yes, we would open ourselves up to rejection, but it's in this space where we also find connection, kindness, and relationship.

Imagine if Lucas put all the energy he used for counterproductive questioning toward solving his shoulder problem. He was a brilliant inventor, after all. The questions that occupied him may have blocked him from receiving the solutions to his problem—a problem many others in the world also have.

Each of us carries a solution to one of the world's problems. Our counterproductive habits prevent those solutions from coming to us. Recognizing our value is the first step in solving the problem for which we alone have the solution.

THE BRIDGE

Indiana couldn't see the bridge. He had to imagine it in order to take the first step. He had to see it in his mind's eye when it was invisible to his normal sight. He had to imagine it would be there to meet his feet if he stepped out into the dark abyss.

The process of moving forward is as much about making peace with the existing story as it is about stopping the actions that recreate negative emotion. It isn't about pretending something isn't true, or a painful event didn't happen. It's about living in the tension of feeling small, unworthy, or unhappy, and then being selective about which stories we choose to think about and tell. Then, it's about what we do to physically stop the negativity from flooding our body with anxiety and depression.

We can literally interrupt a way of thinking by using a creative new thought. The act of designing a new vision for our life is a creative process. When we are facing the invisible bridge, we have the choice to quiet the old thoughts and use our imaginations to create a new outcome. We may have had secondary gains from our most frustrating problem, but if we don't move forward

> Each of us carries a solution to one of the world's problems. Our counterproductive habits prevent those solutions from coming to us. Recognizing our value is the first step in solving the problem for which we alone have the solution.

from it, the world may never receive the solution with which we are uniquely equipped.

Claiming a new story requires faith that we can change our destructive feelings and actions. It's time to quiet our old, internal dialogue and move toward a hope-filled new chapter of our story.

HERE'S WHAT I WOULD SAY TO TREVOR AND TO YOU

During the healing process, you will need to access and reflect on stories that bring positive emotions. Thoughts are like getting in a truck and driving to the neighborhood store. We know which way to go. We could almost do it blindfolded. The brain is wired similarly. It's easy to access certain points of pain and frustration, because we do it often. So we must make different choices.

When you find yourself slipping back into old patterns, you can simply recognize it and take a new, life-affirming action instead. Take this part one day at a time. Don't focus on the times you fail. Focus on your successes. Every positive choice brings you closer to your purpose.

Here are questions for reflection:

1. What habits have you developed that keep you from your goals, such as being healthier, connecting with others, saving money, or getting out of debt?

2. How can you interrupt the thought process that leads you to counterproductive habits?

3. What could you do or say instead?

. . . .

References

1. Beck, M. (n.d.). What an Overweight Former Model Can Teach Us About Breaking Free of Bad Habits. Retrieved October 07, 2018, from http://www.oprah.com/inspiration/martha-beck-explains-how-to-break-free-of-bad-patterns

CHAPTER SIX

STRATEGY #6: CHANGE THE INNER VOICE

———————

"Watch your thoughts, they become words. Watch your words, they become actions. Watch your actions; they become habit. Watch your habits, they become character. Watch your character; it becomes your destiny."

—Lao Tzu

I WAS INTERESTED in knowing more about what was causing my client Mark to continue feeling insignificant. That day, during his coaching call, I asked him about the derogatory names he called himself.

"You want the list?" he responded dryly. "Not good enough, loser, faker, cheater, liar…"

Mark was not alone. In my role as a life coach, I'd heard those same names from hundreds of people.

"They're the words I've heard my whole life," Mark continued.

Growing up, Mark's father was emotionally and verbally abusive to him. He made it clear that Mark could never live up to his standards. Mark felt insignificant.

As an adult, his father continued to criticize Mark for his choices. He wanted Mark to have a traditional nine-to-five job, and Mark's work as a wellness coach and master presenter didn't fit that bill. Mark's lifelong dream was to be an author and to further his career as a presenter. He wanted to write a book and become a public speaker. Mark's father told him he was "chasing dreams" and that his goals were "stupid."

These words affected him on a heart level and damaged his sense of self-worth. They manifested in him as deep feelings of shame and insecurity. And into adulthood, he continued using them in the form of self-talk. Those words became the basis for the language he would use that would continue to damage his identity. They spoke a false narrative that kept him from moving toward his goals.

Mark's mother had always been a buffer between her husband and her son, and when she died, things got even worse. Mark was left to face his father's cruelty without her kindness and support.

It was no wonder Mark struggled with writing a book. If he thought he wasn't good enough, his book wouldn't be good enough. If he felt like a fraud, he believed his book's entire message would be a sham.

As we continued the conversation, it was clear none of the labels Mark's father gave him was accurate. He was intelligent, interesting, and insightful. Personally, I found him a delight to coach.

As a young adult, Mark learned to bury his pain and rejection through overeating and drinking alcohol. Feeling like he didn't have a voice, he replaced being heard with abusing his body.

One morning, Mark woke up knowing he'd been on a binge the night before, but had no recollection of the events that took place. That day, he realized he needed to quit both habits—not only for his own sake, but also for his wife and children. He went into therapy.

Over time, he got sober and began living a healthier lifestyle. He became a fitness professional. But he still had the dream of being an author and motivational speaker. At this point, he'd become accomplished and credentialed as a writer. He'd been published in *The Huffington Post* and other established online publications. But his father's criticism—messages like, "Your book will never sell"—had settled deep in his belief system and held him back from not only writing books but pursuing other opportunities as well. It was like being told he was a failure before he even started.

He couldn't envision taking the next step. Putting himself out there, he'd be risking the kind of criticism he'd heard throughout his childhood. To move forward, he'd have to deliberately silence his father's voice. He'd have to consciously rise above his fears and try anyway. Writing a book would be a tremendous leap of faith.

In one of our coaching conversations, Mark confided, "I've been soul-searching. I've been thinking that if I can help myself, that's how I'll be able to help others." That's when I explained that when facing our next step, before we take it, we tend to ask ourselves three things:

1. Can I do it? (An issue of identity)

2. Is it enough? (An issue of personal value)

3. Will it work? (An issue of faith in self)

Identity affirming words become the figurative soil from which our dreams grow. Just like if the soil of a garden is not fertile, the plant will struggle in the growth process. Negative self-talk and negative beliefs about ourselves have strong correlations with early childhood and past experiences, but can be intentionally stopped and replaced with affirming words. Then, we can nurture our vision for a better tomorrow, and our dreams take root.

IDENTITY – CAN I DO IT?

Personal identity is who we are on the inside and subsequently what we do with our lives. When that identity has a positive voice, we believe we can impact the world through our contributions. We have hope, set challenging goals, and our actions line up with what we believe. If navigated intentionally, the end result is that we leave a legacy for future generations.

However, when we experience trauma and are assaulted with messages that pierce our sense of worthiness on the level of identity, we may continue to cling to the belief that we aren't worthy of love and that we have no purpose. Until we can begin to believe we can be flawed and lovable, imperfect and also acceptable, that we make mistakes and yet we have something inside of us that can change the world, we will not feel contentment or be able to move toward our big dreams. The idea that we can't measure up to an inner ideal standard causes us to stay isolated from others. We hide our gifts and talents under a veneer. We privately wonder if we have what it takes to achieve our lifelong dream.

Identity affirming words become the figurative soil from which our dreams grow.

Words, whether thought or spoken, can keep us imprisoned. Words we use, words we think, words we believe, shape our present-tense ability to foster connection and to charter a course toward our big dreams. Our words are the manifestation of our inner beliefs about our ability to make a difference on the planet. They can cause us to shrink back instead of boldly stepping into the fullness of our identity.

Even after we align with our identity as a world-changer, we may still have to rise above any fear we encounter along the journey. We choose thoughts and words that partner with faith instead of fear.

For example, someone who believes they can help change the world through writing, like Mark, has to overcome their fear of writing and publishing a book. He would have to practice writing despite the inner voice that says he's a fake and will never be a success. When the time was right, he would move forward with his book, expecting the best.

We won't always get our craft down perfectly the first time. We may have to try more than once to get it right. We have to lean into our identity as world changer, someone with a gift that needs to be shared for the betterment of others—and expose ourselves to possible failure and criticism all over again.

PERSONAL VALUE – IS IT ENOUGH?

The next hurdle we'll encounter while pursuing our dreams is the question: "Is it enough?" This question is really less about what we're doing and more about who we are. The real, underlying question is: "Am *I* enough?"

In quiet times of self-reflection, we may wonder if our accomplishments, our work, our contribution to relationships, are enough. At the root of our questioning, we are really asking ourselves, "Am I enough because of who I am and what I've done?" There is always an opportunity to feel like we don't measure up. The words we choose to believe will directly impact what we do next. We will accomplish what we believe we are worth.

FAITH IN SELF – WILL IT WORK?

To diminish the resounding impact of this question, we have to focus on who we are instead of who we're not. Negative thoughts become negative words, which lead to disillusionment. Positive thoughts become positive words and generally lead to faith in ourselves. Unless interrupted, negative cycles will continue and positive cycles will never have the chance to bloom. It's an act of will to change the cycle.

It's like a dripping faucet. The drip will eventually fill the cup. Are we partnering with faith or fear? Are we dripping positive affirmations or criticism? Today's efforts may pay off, or they may give us a point of reference from which to learn. Either way, they are not wasted.

To develop faith in ourselves, we need a big vision with steps that we believe we can accomplish. We adjust our internal language. If we have a negative self-image, we have to change the dialogue. We choose an intentional inner dialogue like, "You will make it this time. You are destined for great things. Your work matters, and your creativity is important."

To develop a vision, we have to go back to our dreams, remind ourselves of how we want to impact the world, and then take simple steps forward. The key is returning to a central belief that we have something inside of ourselves that needs to be shared. We continually realign our daily actions with that vision.

CHOOSING TO LISTEN TO ENCOURAGING WORDS

Two internal voices are usually competing for our attention. One says, "Great things are ahead." The other says, "If you take the next step, you'll fail, and you'll always be a failure." The voice we listen to when we wake up in the morning will usually have control over our feelings and actions that day. Over time, our collection of feelings and actions will either lead to our desired destiny or keep us stuck. It's hard to have faith in ourselves when we feel like we'll never achieve our dreams.

At some point, we'll believe our inner dialogue, even if it started with someone else's negative words, because we continue to repeat it. That's when we stagnate. If we don't intentionally tune in to the positive voice, negativity and anxiety may become the guide for our actions and our life.

The critical words we use about our behavior, our accomplishments, and ourselves can form a wall around our heart—especially during times of uncertainty. That wall will prevent us from sharing our self and moving into our greatest destiny.

The barrier Mark used to protect himself from his father also prevented him from moving forward in life. He described his wall as "very big, with wires and flood lights." It was built to keep people out. But it also trapped pain in.

Taking down the wall would require new dialogue—one fueled by belief in himself. He would need to stop identifying with the 8-year-old boy who'd been verbally abused—the boy who had no voice, no say in his life—and step outside his comfort zone. He'd have to start his book, and move toward his other big goals, despite the disempowering inner dialogue that was still running. He had to begin the process while he still felt doubtful. He had to begin without knowing how things would turn out. He wouldn't start with a sense of accomplishment. That would come over time. He'd have to stop listening to negative internal voices and stop accepting defining labels that undermined his identity as a writer, speaker, and leader.

He simply had to take the next step.

I assured him that the confidence he needed would build along the way. Taking action would diminish his uncomfortable feelings. As he progressed through each step, his belief in himself and his abilities would strengthen.

About a year after our coaching sessions, Mark had become a regional manager for a major fitness corporation. Although he hadn't started his book yet, he was very satisfied with the direction he was headed. By helping others achieve a healthier lifestyle, and helping other fitness professionals with their career goals, he was moving toward his purpose and making a positive difference in the lives of others.

A CHANGE

Just like I told the boys at C.A.M.P., each of us has to first stop the flow of negative words around our beliefs about ourselves. It is a gradual transition. We have to become aware that the words spoken to us, along with past events, influence how we think about ourselves and how we interact with others. We begin to understand how a feeling of rejection may have been guiding our lives. Then we allow a new truth to emerge.

This truth is rooted in the idea that we are enough, just as we are—flawed and imperfectly perfect. It's a truth we have to continuously choose to align with. It doesn't mean we don't have moments where we slip back into a comfortable, small way of thinking; it means we recognize the symptoms of toxic thinking and then realign with thoughts that end in self-compassion.

We begin by believing that we are personally enough, skilled enough, to take the next steps despite our insecurities.

It isn't an accomplishment, wealth, or position at someone else's company that can change our inner beliefs. It is an inside job. For some of us, that means it's a slow and steady desire to stop aligning with years of self-abuse. It is finally time to put our best foot forward despite our flaws and limitations.

The point where we will start truly believing in ourselves is when we decide to move forward knowing we might not do it perfectly—we might even fail. This is also when we realize that everything we've been through—past experiences, jobs, and pain—make sense. We realize none of it was lost. It was all part of something greater. We begin by taking baby steps toward our vision.

MOVING FORWARD DESPITE THE CRITICS

Born in 1965 to a Jewish family that had migrated from Eastern Europe, Ben Stiller grew up with his parents traveling to put on live comedy shows on *The Ed Sullivan Show* and in nightclubs. Stiller jokes, "If my parents were plumbers, who knows what I would be doing now?"2

He wasn't always as self-assured as he is now. "I had moments of real awkwardness and feeling totally outside the loop in terms of being accepted," said Stiller. "I was into theater, but I wasn't a theater nerd—I was somewhere in the middle, having crushes on girls and not feeling worthy, trying to figure out who I was."7 Despite his personal insecurities, Stiller took a step toward his passion for storytelling. He created his own short films with Super 8 cameras, and later took on various small acting parts before landing a stage role in the Tony-award winning theater production, *The House of Blue Leaves*.3

His initial decade of work in no way foretold the mega success story he would later become. In an interview, he explained, "[It] was a weird development process, and I was just trying to figure it out. Then all of a sudden you do a couple of comedies, and that's that. It defines who you are and how people see you."4

His career took a meandering path from creating short films to television to stage. He dropped out of the University of California nine months after starting, and instead took acting classes. Two years later, he made his debut film role in *Fresh Horses*, starring Molly Ringwald and Andrew McCarthy. "Bad, bad, bad, stunningly bad," said one Rotten Tomatoes critic review of the 1988 film.6 She wasn't his only critic.

It would be a full 10 years after that role before Stiller would land the starring role in *There's Something about Mary*, a film that had combined gross sales of more than $369 million.8 Following this blockbuster, Stiller went on to become an A-list talent, acting, directing, producing, and appearing in more than 100 productions that have combined gross revenue earnings in the billions.1 He's starred in movies such as *Night at The Museum* and *Meet The Fockers*, and produced *Zoolander*, *Starsky and Hutch*, and *Dodgeball*.1

The point? Ben Stiller was not an overnight success. He used each performance as an opportunity to refine his craft and not to define his limits—and he didn't listen to his critics. He continued to believe in himself and pursue his passion, trying various avenues and opportunities, over and over again, until the fruit of his success matched his internal belief about what he could achieve. He was a success on the inside before he became a success on the outside.

SELF-FULLFILLING WORDS

In the midst of uncertainty, exhaustion, or shame, we have the choice to partner with fear or faith. Changing the inner dialogue starts when we're ready to let go of our powerless and defeated self-image. We do this through our words and beliefs about our future and ourselves.

If we hang onto damaging words, we won't move toward our dreams. Our actions will reflect our beliefs and words. The stories we replay in our minds will reinforce how we already feel. The messages leave us feeling small, angry, or frozen, and prevent us from tapping into our potential.

Adopting a positive vision starts with boundaries. They don't just keep us safe around other people. We need them in our own thoughts when we're feeling uncertain about the future or shame about the past. We have to disconnect the judgmental inner voice that prevents us from taking positive action. At first, we may continue to hear it, but we have to move forward anyway.

Standing in the presence of insecurity means we may have to be selective about which words influence our decisions. We must grab onto a new powerful identity. We must begin to use words that agree with a new, future vision of ourselves.

Building positive momentum requires us to use motivating words. It means we focus on and talk about how we can and will succeed and then, like Stiller, it means we keep trying. When we revisit words that align with our fear of failure, we can simply acknowledge them and remind ourselves to choose a new ending.

Stepping into our purpose happens over time. Many people who've accomplished great things only did so after countless unsuccessful attempts. Thomas Edison didn't create the light bulb his first try, his hundredth, or even his thousandth. Can you imagine what people might have said about him? What if he had listened to ridicule or skepticism and gave up? What if he had called himself a "failure" and quit before he finally succeeded?

He chose not to think that way. He said, "I have not failed… I have just found ten thousand ways that won't work."[5] It's through persistence and silencing the negative voices that we produce new fruit.

THE INVISIBLE BRIDGE OVER THE CHASM

A chasm lies in front of each of us. It looms over all our interactions with others and our attempts at new experiences. There are heart-pounding, doubt-filled first, second, and third steps we must take into the unknown before we get to the metaphorical other side of the invisible bridge. What we tell ourselves throughout the process is key.

It's time to tell ourselves something new. Like Edison, we may have found 10,000 ways that won't work. But we are not failures.

It's time to try again.

HERE'S WHAT I WOULD SAY TO TREVOR AND TO YOU

You are going to feel this step deeply. You will have to act counter to how you feel inside. This is the step where you have to tune in to the voice that says good things are in store for you. This is where you begin making new decisions based on hope and purpose.

Remember to focus on the end goal while feeling the temporary pain of wading through your deep-rooted insecurities. To find the success you're seeking, you must step, and step again, even if you stumble or fall flat on your face. When you begin to call yourself names, realize they're only a symptom of fear and insecurity. They're an attempt to mask pain. They are not truth. You must stop agreeing with that voice. Moving forward will require you to step bravely into the new while still feeling vulnerable. You've got this. You can and you will!

Here are questions for reflection:

1. What names are you calling yourself? When do you call yourself these names?

2. What is something positive that you could say when you're feeling negative emotion?

3. What is one goal or dream you would pursue if you decided to stop telling yourself you would never succeed?

. . . .

References

1. Ben Stiller. (n.d.). Retrieved July 2, 2019, from https://www.imdb.com/name/nm0001774/

2. Ben Stiller. (n.d.). Retrieved July 1, 2019, from https://www.jewishvirtual-library.org/ben-stiller

3. Ben Stiller Biography. (Biography.com Editors). (2014, April 2). Ben Stiller Biography. Retrieved July 1, 2019, from https://www.biography.com/actor/ben-stiller

4. Brooks, X. (2008, September 18). 'I wish people didn't see me like that'. Retrieved July 1, 2019, from https://www.theguardian.com/film/2008/sep/19/benstiller.comedy

5. Furr, N. (2011, August 09). How Failure Taught Edison to Repeatedly Innovate. Retrieved July 1, 2019, from

https://www.forbes.com/sites/nathanfurr/2011/06/09/
how-failure-taught-edison-to-repeatedly-innovate/#60bfa07165e9

6. Ketron, L. (2019, June 25). Fresh Horses (1988). Retrieved July 1, 2019, from https://www.rottentomatoes.com/m/fresh_horses

7. Shone, T. (2010, May 28). Ben Stiller: 'I never talk to my shrink about comedy'. Retrieved July 2, 2019, from https://www.theguardian.com/film/2010/may/29/ben-stiller-interview-shrink-comedy

8. There's Something About Mary (1998). (n.d.). Retrieved July 1, 2019, from https://www.boxofficemojo.com/movies/?id=somethingaboutmary.htm

THIRD LIFE LESSON: CULTIVATE A CLIMATE OF CONNECTION

RELEASED IN 1997, the movie *Good Will Hunting* is about a math prodigy, Will Hunting, who was physically abused as a child.[2] Now a 20-year-old high school dropout, he works as a janitor for the prestigious Massachusetts Institute of Technology (MIT). Working the night shift, Will solves the extremely complex math problems posted on a bulletin board by Professor Gerald Lambeau for his students. When Gerald discovers that Will is the one solving them, he wants to get a sense of how Will's mind works. He wants to spend time with him in math brainstorming sessions, but first he needs to help keep Will, who had assaulted a police officer, out of prison.

At the court hearing, at Gerald's request, Will receives a deferred sentence in exchange for agreeing to study with the professor and to go into therapy. Gerald has a therapist in mind—Sean, a 20-year counseling veteran and former college roommate of Gerald's.

Will's connection with Gerald and Sean gives him both a venue to express his mathematical genius and the chance he needs to find acceptance and love.

In one scene, Will arrives for his therapy session to find Sean and Gerald arguing.[1] When they see Will, they stop abruptly. Gerald leaves, and Will walks in.

"A lot of that stuff goes back a long way between me and him, you know," Sean says, referring to his complicated history with Gerald. "It's not about you."

His last statement would unintentionally set the tone for a breakthrough that would change Will's life. "It's not about you" would become "It's not your fault."

During this session, Will discovers his own patient file and rifles through it. Among its contents are photos of the bruises his foster father had inflicted on him.

Looking through Sean's notes, Will is trying to figure out the therapist's motives for working with him. He's not interested in Sean's clinical experience treating pain. He wants to know if Sean has any personal experience with the kind of abuse Will had endured— whether Sean can feel his pain or is only diagnosing his actions. He wants to know if Sean is interested in him as a subject or as a friend.

Sean moves closer to Will. "You see this?" he says, gazing into Will's eyes warmly, referring to the photos. "All this stuff? It's not your fault." He pauses and repeats the words. "It's not your fault." He continues repeating this phrase until the words break through the emotional barrier that Will has erected to shut out people and pain. He buries his face in his hands and begins to weep. In that moment, Will reveals his pain long enough to let healing enter his heart.

So many of us carry around words, moments, actions, and emotional or physical abuse. Horrific incidents may have deeply penetrated our hearts. Even though the bruises are no longer visible, the pain may have caused us to back away from relationships and to stay isolated.

Those events were not our fault. They happened to us. We didn't seek trauma, being yelled at or abused, nor to be treated unkindly or unfairly. Long after the moment has passed, we're presented with an option: Either feel the pain and let it go, or grab it and hold onto it.

What keeps us safe also keeps us isolated.

Pain elicits a response. It may cause us to create a veneer of perfection or to withdraw from social activities. Many of us draw a boundary around the place where we store the pain.

It's true, it happened. It wasn't our choice to get hurt. However, it is our choice to heal.

HOW TO MOVE FORWARD

This next section is dedicated to dealing with the obstacles to building healthy relationships and sharing the song that lives in each of us. Relationships are the central component of developing a strong sense of worthiness. Learning to connect is a vital part of living a purpose-filled life. The next chapters are about letting go of the old to make room for the new, with a focus on how to end behavior that leads to disconnection.

We'll look at how to recognize our participation in the cycle that has blocked emotional well-being and prevented us from feeling loved. Chapter 7 tackles the first few steps to establishing healthy connections. In Chapter 8, we learn to recognize how we've closed ourselves off, so that we can choose to make new decisions to be known and loved. Chapter 9 revisits overcoming unhealthy response patterns.

We all have moments of wanting to retreat. Commitment to letting go of what no longer serves us and to developing positive relationships is part of the process of restoring hope. When we learn the art of connection, we will be able to more readily develop a sense of balance and purpose. This type of change comes at a personal cost, since it means we have to risk being known. We can't produce our symphony alone. Building relationships and letting love in is a life-long learning process of trying again after falling flat on our face, and making room in our lives to establish—or re-establish—trust and connection.

. . . .

References

1. Famous Movie Scene: Good Will Hunting "It's Not Your Fault" HD. (2011, August 24). Retrieved November 28, 2017, from https://www.youtube.com/watch?v=UYa6gbDcx18

2. Good Will Hunting Full Cast & Crew. (n.d.). Retrieved November 28, 2017, from http://www.imdb.com/title/tt0119217/fullcredits/

CHAPTER SEVEN

STRATEGY #7: LET IT GO

═══════════

"No one can make you feel inferior without your consent."

– Eleanor Roosevelt

"IT'S WHEN I'M alone with my thoughts that the situation really starts getting me down," she began. "I feel guilty when I'm not there."

Erin was referring to her estranged relationship with her sister, Kacie, and brother-in-law, Jay. She no longer visited their home. Jay had been unfaithful to Kacie, and it upset Erin deeply. Erin and Kacie had always been close, and when Kacie was hurt, Erin took it to heart.

Kacie had decided to forgive her husband and work things out with him. But Erin was still upset about it. To Erin, forgiving Jay would be like approving of his transgression. She was so resentful about it, she stopped communicating with them both, causing a bitter rift in her relationship with Kacie.

"I'm sad about what his actions have done to our family," Erin said. "I miss the old normal." The way she described it, it was more than sadness—it seemed all-consuming. She'd been thinking about it every day.

As her coach, my job was to help her look at the story objectively and get to the root of the problem.

"What if Jay's behavior wasn't an issue for you?" I asked.

This was a hard question to ask of someone who had a high standard of ethics and a deep love for her family. She paused before answering.

"To make that happen, I would have to be the bigger person," she replied. "Not letting it drag me down would be the harder choice."

I told her that we have to choose to let go in order to move forward. Internalizing negativity keeps us small and isolated. Whether to move past the hurtful behaviors of others or to hold onto them is a choice we make. Internalizing these experiences is like stuffing them into a big bag and dragging that bag around with us wherever we go. Everyone we meet senses the contents of our bag, whether we openly show them or not. For Erin, continually revisiting her brother-in-law's behavior was adding weight to her bag.

As we talked, Erin began to realize that dragging around Jay's issues was counterproductive. His problems were not something she was required to bear. Although letting go would take time, she realized that it would be in her own best interest. Allowing his actions to define her sense of well-being was an act of futility.

Holding someone hostage for their hurtful behavior requires a massive amount of energy and leaves us emotionally exhausted. It causes dissension, bitterness, heartache, and pain for us—not for them. Revisiting those behaviors does not bring justice. And Erin also needed to see the other side of that coin: Releasing them doesn't give them our stamp of approval. Choosing forgiveness would not be endorsing Jay's transgressions. But it would release her from the pain.

The walls we build around ourselves keep us from living a full, connected life. When we cut off the flow of one relationship with bitterness or anger, it impacts our other relationships. Likewise, when we forgive one person, we can begin to develop deeper, healthier connections with others.

But it's not only the big moments that can cause ruptures in our relationships. Small, private wounds can also require forgiveness. And if not treated similarly to the larger ones, they can have the same lasting impact on our lives and emotional well-being.

IMPERFECTIONS

I was able to say goodbye to my grandfather before he passed. My cousin put him on FaceTime so I could relive some memories with him.

"Remember taking me back home with you to Arizona?" I'd asked in a high-pitched voice, choking back a sob. Without first checking with my parents, I had begged my grandparents to take me on the 12-hour trip back to their house in Glendale, just outside of Phoenix—and they did.

While traveling, my grandfather had pulled over in the middle of the highway. I heard his booming voice from the back of the motor home. "Which way we gonna go, ma?" he'd asked my grandmother.

I can't remember why I thought it was funny. But it felt special to watch the moment as I walked around the back of the RV. It was like a TV comedy.

He died at 4 a.m. the next morning.

At the funeral, the pastor summarized my grandfather's life. His father—my great-grandfather—had died when my grandfather was a young boy. With only a third grade education, he dropped out of school to work on the farm and help feed his brothers, sister and mother. He tried to join the military when he was 16, but they didn't enlist him until he was a couple of years older. He would have been drafted had he not volunteered to join. In the Marines, he served as an infantryman who operated a flamethrower on the hills of Okinawa in World War II. When he came home, he became a truck driver.

My dad experienced the brunt of my grandfather's violent episodes. He was beaten with whatever was at hand—an iron, a belt buckle, tree switches. "How do you like that?" my grandfather would sneer as the object repeatedly ripped into my dad's flesh. My dad endured beatings that left blood running down his legs, welts all over his body, and eyes swollen shut.

The grandfather I had experienced was a softer, more contained personality. Much to the dismay of my father, I adored him.

His funeral portrayed both the light and shadows of his life.

The pastor closed the funeral with a story. "There is a certain kind of fighter jet that flies at a very high altitude. However, when it's on the ground, it leaks oil. The plane wasn't meant to sit; its job is done in the air, where the pressure kept the closures tight." He used this story as a way to bring the extremes together and healing to those listening. The inner grit that helped my grandfather withstand losing his childhood to farm labor and the horrors of war caused him to inflict deep pain in others that he loved. When he was at home, he leaked.

The deep dysfunction of my grandfather's abuse led to a cycle of self-abuse in my dad. He drank to numb his feelings and gave way to perfectionist tendencies. When he was triggered, he yelled until veins stood out on his neck.

One day, I caught myself yelling at my own son. Disgusted, I vowed I would never do it again. Instead, I turned toward perfectionism and control. They kept me from the deeper relationships I desired with others. I continued to abuse myself with these habits until I became aware that I was leaking, too. The only way to end the leak was to refit the plane for a new mission: connection with others.

Forgiveness had to start with others and end with forgiving myself.

DEEP FORGIVENESS

The first time I had to work hard toward total forgiveness was with my dad. It's a continual process of letting go. First, I forgave him for his actions during my adolescent years, and then for the fresh wounds he'd inflicted as an adult.

Next, I worked toward slowly releasing my deep-rooted insecurities and shame. I decided my dad would always be part of my life, but his rage and hurtful words wouldn't. I could feel the heaviness and sadness of memories for a moment, and then choose to gently release it.

Forgiveness was the first step of my healing. Creating healthy boundaries was the second. I stopped holding my dad's actions accountable for my well-being, but I also stopped allowing myself to be berated and yelled at—by anyone.

The third step was owning my feelings and new boundaries while establishing a new, deeper relationship with my father. I was fortunate to get that opportunity. He had reduced his drinking to the occasional glass of wine and had stopped raging. He became kinder and more interested in my life. I learned to focus on the good times instead of the bad. Happy memories co-existed with the painful stories. For instance, when my brother and I were children, my dad took us on many fun outings—for donuts, to the local café, skiing on the lake, to Yosemite, camping, and countless vacations. I not only had to forgive, but to remind myself of those positive experiences.

During a visit, I told my dad how much I appreciated all the things he had done for our family. He stayed at a stressful job to provide for us. Although he grew up so poor that he had to shower outside with a hose, he had afforded my family life in a nice neighborhood. Although he'd been beaten as a child, he refrained from that level of physical violence toward us. He did the best he could with what he was given.

It was as though I had the chance to start where he had finished. Life hadn't been perfect for me either, but it was time for a generational shift. Forgiveness would start with me. I pursued inner healing so I could have a relationship with my dad, and I would not carry the abuse forward with my own children or with myself.

I made a deliberate choice that for the rest of my dad's life, I would get to know him by listening to his stories and loving him as he is in the present moment. I've opted to allow him to stand in the middle of his pain but have chosen to release mine. I worked toward extending love instead of judgment.

It was one of the best decisions I've ever made.

A DELIBERATE CHOICE

It was a deliberate choice for me to focus on the positive. Like it was for Erin. As it is for each of us.

Joyce Meyer, author, speaker and president of her own ministry, says, "Staying angry at someone who has hurt you is like taking poison hoping that your enemy will die." We will experience the emotions we don't release. When we hold onto someone else's anger or bitterness, we stay angry or bitter. Those emotions, unless intentionally released, will become the foundation for our life going forward.

For our song to become a symphony, we cannot play in isolation. The very act of "playing" can expose us to hurtful situations and can keep us silent. Some of us don't play our song because we're afraid to fail in front of others. We make excuses for why we won't try again, but it's really to self-protect.

Forgiveness is only the first part of the process. We must learn to choose a new pattern of thinking by focusing on the good in life, and on the positive, instead of the negative. The process isn't easy. It breaks down into four phases.

Phase One: Let it Go

The first phase is to identify what, or whom, we have allowed to rob us of our peace. It may be an event or a person. It goes back to the bag of our harmful experiences. When we carry fear, anger, negativity, disappointment, ugliness, or unkindness with us, we drag it around in our bag. If we're not in control of our own sense of well-being, chances are we still need to open the door to forgiveness. We don't need to contact that person for the process to begin. This process is not about them. It's about us.

We can simply repeat these words to ourselves: "I choose to forgive _____ for _____."
Again, the person we forgive may truly be at fault, and forgiving them may be one of the toughest things we will ever have to do. It is not about whether they were wrong or right. It's about stopping their actions from robbing us of our confidence and peace. It keeps "their thing" from being "our thing." When we forgive them, their problem becomes solely "their thing." Letting go of the offense begins the process of healing. It's about regaining the space we have allowed them to occupy in our hearts.

Phase Two: Let Ourselves Off the Hook

Phase two is about taking ownership of the emotions that prevent us from connecting with others. We have to choose to live an empowered life. We stop residing in a reactionary mode and begin to make conscious decisions about our actions and relationships. We become deliberate. We start by taking one vulnerable step—and then another—toward healthy relationships and goals.

We also use the same process of forgiveness toward ourselves. If we made bad decisions in the past, we let ourselves off the hook for those choices. Very often, it's easier to ask others to forgive us than to forgive ourselves. Owning responsibility for our life gives us the freedom to live from a place of power.

Phase Three: Create Healthy Boundaries

Phase three is about setting boundaries. Instead of interacting with someone else's problems, we decide what works for us. We don't borrow issues from the past or imagine what could happen in the future. We stay present with life as it's happening. Other people may project their pain and feelings of worthlessness onto us as anger, control, and manipulation, but we can draw lines—instead of building walls.

Boundaries with someone who we feel wronged us in a social situation are very different from the kind we need when someone perpetrates violence against us. Creating a plan of action to establish personal safety is an absolute priority. If someone is emotionally abusing us, our boundaries need to include specific rules that limit interaction.

We have to define what we will tolerate.

We choose to see ourselves as a powerful driver of our own story. When we become an actor instead of a reactor, we own our personal worthiness and can choose to move past offenses.

Phase Four: Change the Narrative

We need to study the stories we tell ourselves during moments of deep insecurity. Like Erin, we need to stop focusing on the familiar, negative cycle of thought so we can change how we feel. That means we consciously stop interacting with other people's "bags" and embracing them as our own. Those old stories can keep us from letting people get to know us and forming lasting connections. Changing the story doesn't mean we pretend the past hasn't happened; it means we choose to NOT view other people's problems and unkindness as a running narrative about what's possible for us.

Even if we are doing everything to the best of our ability, someone will eventually say or do something that causes disequilibrium. Although it may initially cause us to feel small and back away, it's what we decide next that matters.

RISK BEING KNOWN

When we choose not to accept other people's issues as our own, it means we stop living small, isolated lives, and learn how to reconnect and risk being known. Being known sets the stage for being loved and valued.

We need to purposefully move toward people with whom we can safely and courageously share our life.

Connection and a sense of community are built over time. We cannot force relationship. We will most likely be at different levels of connection with different people. We need to allow for simple points of connection. Most often, connection is intentional. For example, it's a water-cooler conversation at work, or picking up the phone to say "hi" to an old friend. It could occur when we show up at our children's school or at church events. This part of the process can only happen when we stop focusing inwardly and reach out. We begin to tell our stories.

> When we become an actor instead of a reactor, we own our personal worthiness and can choose to move past offenses.

The group of friends and family in whom we place our trust will most likely be fewer than five people. They are our "tribe." These are the people who will stand by us when we risk being known, the ones to whom we can show our pain and who will hear us without judgment. We may have pieced this group together over time, and they may not live nearby, but they are our tribe nonetheless. If we haven't developed our tribe, it may be time to reach out to a few potential connections and move forward with intentionality.

HERE'S WHAT I WOULD SAY TO TREVOR AND TO YOU

The symphony that lives inside you can only play when you let other people off the hook for the pain they created in your life. And when you do, it gives you the chance to form new connections from a healthier place. You only need to resolve the conflict inside you—not with the other person. You can simultaneously choose to set a boundary with the person who wronged you until they prove to be trustworthy—at which point you can move toward a more healthy relationship one step at a time.

When you allow the healing of forgiveness to set in, it opens the door to change—in yourself, your relationships, and your life. Setting boundaries is healthy and reasonable for establishing what will and won't work. Doing so comes from a place of complete worthiness. A boundary is not a wall; it's a way to connect and to protect your heart. Boundaries will help let the right people in and keep the wrong people, and stories, out.

Questions for reflection:

1. Have you embraced anyone else's problems as your own?

2. How would your life change if a situation where you were wronged no longer impacted you?

3. What boundaries need to be set in place for you to move forward in that relationship?

CHAPTER EIGHT

STRATEGY #8:
LET LOVE IN

"You have been criticizing yourself for years, and it hasn't worked. Try approving of yourself and see what happens."

– Louise L. Hay

SHE WAS DAYS away from relocating her fitness business and fatigue was setting in. "I wish I was in the new space already," she sighed.

It was the Christmas season, and although Kate was tired of living in limbo, things were moving along nicely. Thanks to a lot of recent publicity, people were learning about her training services. She had high hopes for the new year.

From an outside perspective, she was doing amazingly well. She was committed to her marriage. She had a thriving business, and a fit, healthy body. But she felt she worked too much, so in our session, she wanted to talk about finding balance.

"I want to be involved in lots of different things," she said. "I need to figure out my priorities."

We started down her list. "I like working, but I want to feel like I can step away," she said. "I need to take care of myself. For example, I'd like to have nights off, so I have more time to devote to my faith and my husband. But I'm afraid people will be disappointed. Still, I need to learn how to say 'no.'"

Her feelings were understandable. Each morning, she woke up early, led classes and training sessions all day, did her own workout in between sessions, and taught more classes at night. She wanted more time for herself, but she believed that if she hired other teachers for some of these classes, she'd be letting her clients down. "I feel like it would make me less of a trainer," she said.

This point tapped into one of her core values—her sense of self-worth. Her identity was based on other people's perceptions of her instead of on her essential self, and it drove her to try and be perfect. "Being a trainer is part of who I am," she said. "If I cut back on time or classes, I would feel like I failed somehow."

After a pause, I asked, "Do you let people love you?" It was a 180-degree shift from the topic.

"It's hard for me," she replied, "because of my fear of getting hurt." I pointed out that doing so would require that she drop her veneer of perfection and allow herself to be vulnerable. Later, she would tell me that this question hit her like a ton of bricks. "It struck my soul," she said.

Kate had been independent since the day she was born, according to her parents. She was two weeks late, they said, and had been doing things her way ever since.

As high-achievers, Kate's parents expected her to maintain a certain level of excellence, including making straight A's in school and maintaining a specific weight. The body issue stemmed from the fact that Kate's mother's side of the family had always been overweight. Growing up, Kate's thinner sister was showered with more attention. Kate's jealousy became a source of conflict and tension.

During her first year of college, Kate gained 15 pounds. Her mother decided to try and "help" her daughter by offering her money to lose the extra weight. This, Kate said, was when she came to believe that love was conditional. The message Kate received from this was that to be loved, she needed to be perfect.

Internalizing this definition of love led Kate to restrict her food intake, which resulted in an eating disorder. She didn't feel worthy, pretty or wanted. She overcame the disorder when she became a fitness professional, but instead of losing the need for control, she channeled it into over-exercising and overworking. Now, in our sessions, she was ready to find harmony between work, family, and spiritual life. I wondered how she would feel about giving her schedule some breathing space instead of living such an intensely busy life.

"How would you change your goals if you believed you were already loved—as though being loved was automatic, and not dependent on anything you did or said?" I asked.

"That's a foreign idea," she replied. "It would require vulnerability and an admission that I'm only human. Trust and vulnerability—those are scary things for me." Then she paused to think about how her life might specifically change. "I wouldn't teach at night. I would devote my time after 2 p.m. to writing my book and blog posts."

It sounded to me as though she would be trading one busy task for another, which still didn't leave time for the things she'd mentioned—family and spirituality.

This is when I described The Six Archetypes, a model I designed to display less than desirable dynamics of human behavior. Each represents a different behavioral response we might develop for coping with our experiences. At some time in our life, these patterns protected us from unsafe circumstances. For instance, if our parents, schoolmates or spouses were angry, self-centered, or abusive, we probably felt scared, hurt, unloved, unseen, or unimportant. As a result, we may have developed these protective shields. Now, we feel the pain of a double-bind. We want the connection—to be seen and loved—but our responses keep us closed off.

The cycle that started with self-protection led to a swirling wheel of perfectionism, excessive control, caustic attitudes, and other behaviors that kept us distant from relationships and numbed us from the joy and happiness we so desired. These archetypes are metaphors that help us view our behavioral patterns with more objectivity.

The archetypal characters are:

- The Vagabond – the separatist
- The Hunter – the manager
- The Prey – the wounded
- The Achiever – the adventurer
- The Tourist – the perfectionist
- The Traveler – the adapter

The Vagabond is the loner who chooses not to make any lasting connections. He is suspicious of other people's motives, and believes life is rough and something to escape. In fact, escaping the harsh reality of life is a constant part of the Vagabond's life. He has few possessions and even fewer friends. Relationships with others are ruled by sarcasm and reflecting on the hardships of life. The Vagabond's dream is to find an isolated house, off the grid and away from other people who could cause him pain.

Unlike the Vagabond, **The Hunter** enjoys social situations she feels she can manage and control. She believes feelings of unworthiness and pain can be avoided if situations are handled the right way. The Hunter always has a calculated plan, which includes organizing her life and the lives around her. Choice words are readily unleashed when the Hunter perceives lack of control. Her dream is to live in an orderly space where she can minimize interaction with anyone who might disrupt the well-established flow.

The Prey lives in constant fear of being victimized by the Hunter. The Prey has been manipulated and controlled by others, and works desperately to keep from being wounded again. He's constantly reacting to the fear of being stalked and attacked. The Prey lives in a thick, brick-lined fortress to avoid further injury. The bricks are reinforcement against enemy fire. Although friendlier than the Vagabond and safer than the Hunter, the Prey's brick walls are his physical and emotional boundaries. His idea of a perfect life is to limit exposure by creating a physically and emotionally safe haven.

The Adventurer's ultimate goal is accomplishment. Rather than put down roots, she's in constant search of the mountaintop. Unlike the Vagabond, she has a base of support, and lives minimally, but in a village with others. Because she's constantly on an adventure, she doesn't have time for connecting with those around her. Conquest gives her a sense of significance. When mountaineering, Adventurers travel light, enabling them to move easily from one mountaintop to the next with the least amount of hindrance. To contrast two of the archetypes, the Adventurer is looking for the achievement while the Vagabond is trying to survive.

Like the Adventurer and the Vagabond, **the Tourist** doesn't dive deeply into formal connections. The Tourist likes to showcase his life in a certain light and therefore presents a well-crafted persona to the world. Living within fortified walls similar to the Prey's, the Tourist carefully limits exposure to others to avoid emotional vulnerability. He keeps his emotions separate or hidden, choosing to highlight aspects of his life that will divert attention from their pain or discontent. The Tourist's idea of a perfect life is one that allows him to create a world where he chooses how others perceive him by perfecting how he will be seen.

Of all the archetypes, **the Traveler** is the most resilient and ready for relationships, because she is open to sharing herself and comfortable being flexible as plans change. The Traveler enjoys being immersed in new surroundings, new ideas, and the diversity of experiences she encounters with different people. Like the Adventurer, the Traveler has a base of support and has deeply rooted connections in the village where she lives. The Traveler embraces life with open arms and learns to build upon positive experiences. She takes risks to step out into the unknown, even after failing.

The main difference between the Traveler and the Adventurer is in where they place significance. For the Traveler, significance comes from a life well lived, and through relationships—which she mainly finds in her village. She has learned to eat like a king when there is plenty and to live humbly when there is little. The Traveler adapts to her surroundings and is not defined by life's valley or mountaintop experiences. Her idea of a perfect life is a connected life.

I turned my attention back to Kate. "Do you identify with any of these characters?"

"I have an addiction to perfection," she confided. "I give people an 'Instagram reel.' I'm a cross between the Adventurer and the Tourist."

Returning to my original question, I asked, "How would you act if you felt you were worthy of love—without having to earn it?"

"I would work less," she said. She realized that she wasn't working 12-hour days just to pay the bills—she did it to feel a sense of significance, which she thought would fill her *with a sense of love.*

Inspired, Kate remarked, "I think that instead of a goal list for next year, I need a personal manifesto." Instead of checking off items on a list, she decided that her life needed to be aligned with her values.

Nearly a year later, Kate was working toward intentionality in her relationships and building her personal brand as a presenter instead of just filling her time training clients. She moved toward community and relationship-building. She also prioritized her personal goals. Instead of going it alone, she pursued them with like-minded friends and teammates.

Two years later, when Kate and her husband filed for divorce, those with whom she'd built a connection helped her through the rocky journey. They were her steadfast tribe. She moved through that chapter in her life like a Traveler—feeling the emotions, but staying connected to the people who offered unconditional love and support.

A CONNECTED LIFE

When we can recognize the cycle that keeps us from living a connected life, we can purposefully begin taking steps outside our comfort zone, where we allow ourselves to be known. There is a tension in allowing people into our lives—being vulnerable, while still maintaining boundaries. We become known by being present—by creating connection in the smallest moments. We allow people in to see past the veneer we have created, one moment at a time. We create space in our schedule for these points of connection to take place. When they see us, they see our imperfections as well as our strengths. We tell our story because we begin to deeply believe we are worthy of being heard. Our connections become part of our symphony. Our song becomes a part of other people's lives.

Instead of trying to endure life like a Vagabond, we turn our focus toward helping others. Valleys—hard times—can present great meaning and insights, but we were never meant to set up camp there and live in sadness. While our circumstances may not change appreciably, we can change the way we think during challenging times. For instance, our life may look the same, but we change on the inside by no longer isolating ourselves. Instead, we move toward healthy connections.

Although it may feel comfortable to hyper-control our circumstances like the Hunter, real connections occur through vulnerability. Instead of erasing our pain, controlling life's circumstances and other people is like damming up the river before the waterfall. It stifles the vulnerability required for relationship. When we can view life and time with others as something to be enjoyed, we can slowly release some of our management and control issues.

We form connections by listening to other points of view. As hard as we try not to, most of us carry past wounds with us. Not everyone with a different point of view is trying to control, manipulate, harm, or abandon us. We can begin to trust others. We can begin to feel positive emotions.

To stop being the Prey, we have to choose to stop feeling victimized by others. Often, as the Prey, we have truly experienced hurt, trauma, and misery at the hands of others. Preventing new wounds around caustic and hurtful people means we must set boundaries. This keeps us from being influenced by someone else's baggage. It gives us room to see what is theirs and what is ours.

Boundaries are different from walls. By gradually showing up and allowing others to see us, and to hear our story, we realize we don't have to self-protect. We are worthy of being seen. We will have to face our fears of feeling like we are not good enough when we risk being seen, heard, and experienced. Over time, by moving past the walls, we will begin to find peace and contentment.

We tell our story because we begin to deeply believe we are worthy of being heard. Our connections become part of our symphony. Our song becomes a part of other people's lives.

Living more like the Traveler and less like the Adventurer means we balance connection with significance. All of us need to feel a sense of significance. However, when we can find it in how we choose to connect, we reprioritize friendships and relationships over achievement. We begin to experience a deeper fulfillment that can only come from heart connections and being seen.

RECOVERY IS AN ACT OF WILL

In her book, *You Are More Than You Know*, international speaker and best-selling author Patsy Clairmont shares her experience of living with paralyzing fear.[1] In her mid 20s, Clairmont was diagnosed with agoraphobia. The American Psychiatric Association defines the condition as "anxiety in situations where the person perceives their environment to be unsafe with no easy way to escape."

Internal terror had claimed her peace. She was panic-stricken, often bedridden, taking up to four tranquilizers a day just to feel like she could survive, and sometimes rushing to the hospital for Demerol, a medication used to calm panic attacks.

When her doctor suggested she attend group meetings for people with anxiety disorders, Clairmont acquiesced out of desperation.

From the first meeting, she felt instant relief in realizing she was not alone. "Knowing I wasn't the only mental muddle, and that others had found a way to survive their panic, gave me a possible path out of my despair," she said. "Hearing them made me feel braver, and they taught me by example that I didn't have to feel courageous to take scary steps forward." After that first meeting, she never took Demerol again.

Clairmont attributes her recovery to her faith, discipline in her thoughts and choices, and her "neighborhood" of friends—the recovery group. "Connecting in life-changing ways with others was healing for me; like opening a window in a stuffy room." Making these connections and learning new coping strategies set her on a path toward recovery.

Instead of riding her tidal wave of emotions, Clairmont leaned into her will to change. She began to alter the way she spoke about herself and the running dialogue in her mind. She learned to identify her feelings. Instead of peering out of the window, pacing and worrying, she practiced "gratitude, generosity, and graciousness." She spent her time studying the scriptures in the Bible, meditating, praying, painting, writing, baking, and resting. She stayed in community with others. Although she says it was "awkward at first," she gradually became less reactive and more positive. She took ownership over her responses toward stressors and continued taking steps out of her restrictive lifestyle.

Clairmont eventually began a career speaking and writing about her experiences. She has now written more than 30 books, spoken at the Pentagon, and was a founding speaker at nationwide Women of

Faith conferences. She has traveled around the world, encouraging millions with her hope-filled, inspiring messages.

RECEIVING LOVE

To find our "neighborhood," we must risk being known. The process means we take steps toward others. We reveal our painful pasts and tell our stories with safe people. We give ourselves room to be imperfect and to make mistakes.

We continue to live with boundaries over our thoughts and actions. We resist the fear of withholding our true self from others. We willfully take steps out of emotional and physical isolation. Through these small steps we begin to establish trust. Connections are formed naturally and we reprioritize our time. We place effort behind becoming friendlier, kinder, more thoughtful, more appreciative, and in doing so we take the focus off ourselves.

Love flows naturally. What stops us from feeling love is how we choose to see the world. Receiving love is an act of vulnerability. We can't manage the flow. Do we see it as a struggling Vagabond—avoiding pain by avoiding people and focusing on our challenges? Do we see it as a controlled Hunter—managing pain by being controlling, or as the Prey, by isolating ourselves and focusing on how we've been wounded? Do we prioritize achievement over connection like the Adventurer? Like the Tourist, do we see it as something to plan and manage so we can hide our feelings and imperfections under a veneer of perfection?

CHOOSING TO BE KNOWN

When we decide to stop worrying about how we might be treated, we can start thinking about how to make other people feel comfortable, seen and appreciated. We can begin by allowing people to see us for who we really are. When we stop worrying about other people's perceptions, it gives us tremendous freedom to focus on loving others instead of worrying, attempting to control situations or manage other people's opinions of us. It also gives us a chance to develop new friendships.

Instead of attempting to make friends, we become friendlier, which draws people to us. Instead of micro-managing our time, we leave some blank spaces to allow for natural conversations to occur and relationships to flourish. Instead of having a rigid, work-oriented purpose, we allow our purpose to include the relationships and experiences of life.

OTHERS FIRST

It is believed that General William Booth, founder of The Salvation Army, sent his employees a one-word telegram that defined his mission.[2]

The telegram stated: "Others."

What might change if each of us acted like we were likeable people and then began sharing parts of ourselves with others? What if we decided to stop worrying about whether people like us or how they see us? What if we made room in our lives for other people and listened to their stories?

When we put others first, we embrace connection. We see ourselves as a contributor to a greater purpose, instead of constantly reacting, trying to manage other people's perceptions of us, and trying to stay emotionally safe. When we let love in, we allow ourselves to belong and to be known. In turn, we give others permission to do the same.

HERE'S WHAT I WOULD SAY TO TREVOR AND TO YOU

Creating a significant life starts with letting love in—with connection. Identifying the ways we isolate is the first step toward learning how to connect. To become fulfilled, we have to find significance not only within our work or activities, but in relationship.

When you clearly understand your patterns, you can end the cycles that cause disconnection. You may find that letting love in is as much of a process as is stopping counterproductive behavior that keeps love out. It calls for a shift in priorities, a new way of thinking, and life-giving, thoughtful behavior. Letting love in also requires you to examine how you create disconnection in your life.

You are lovable. You are worthwhile. It's time your heart overflowed with support and encouragement from people who love you for who you are.

Questions for reflection:

1. Have you been keeping up a veneer of perfection?
2. When do you hide instead of connect?
3. Do you try and manage or control the circumstances?

· ·

References

1. Clairmont, P. (2015). You Are More Than You Know: Face Your Fears, Grow Stronger. Franklin, TN: Worthy Books.

2. Salvation Army Vision. (n.d.). Retrieved July 2, 2019, from https://www.tradeforhope.com/about-others

CHAPTER NINE

STRATEGY #9:
LEARN THE ART
OF CONNECTION

"Only when we are brave enough to explore the darkness
will we discover the infinite power of our light."

– Dr. Brené Brown

"I FEEL LIKE I burned out this past weekend," said Jacob, the business analyst who did part-time work as a personal trainer. "I lost control of my emotions."

It was Jacob's fourth coaching session with me, and he was discussing a situation at work that had caused a problem he'd been struggling with: overreacting. He'd identified it as an ongoing issue for him, and it was putting a strain on his marriage and family.

At his job, he'd been asked to produce a written analysis of a project. After he did, each of his team members reviewed it and added comments to it. Each comment required him to produce additional information—unnecessarily, he felt. He had appreciated the first few comments, but many that followed delivered redundant information, and he felt it had become counterproductive. The cumulative effect brought his emotions to a boiling point and led to severe anxiety.

As we continued talking, Jacob realized why his co-workers' comments were so upsetting: They were seeping into the base layer of how he felt about himself. They made him feel like his initial analysis was a waste of time and that he wasn't good at his job. He defined his self-worth by his work performance. Then, he took those negative feelings home, and they directly impacted his family.

All week, Jacob had been looking forward to Friday family movie night. He needed the downtime. He was even prepared to watch his young daughter's favorite Disney movie. But instead of the movie, she became insistent on watching a TV show she'd been watching for several days—"Peppa Pig."

"When it's on for hours on end, it kind of drives you nuts," he said, adding jokingly, "When is somebody going to turn that pig into bacon?"

His emotions boiled over. He felt that family time wasn't fun for anyone except his daughter. So instead of unwinding with his family, he decided to blow off steam by going upstairs to watch a movie alone.

Unfortunately, the same cycle of frustration repeated itself the next day and ended with Jacob being alone at the gym. By Monday morning, his behavior had caused a strain on his marriage. He was concerned.

By the time of our session, he had bounced back from the negativity, but he wanted to learn from the experience. His homework from the previous session was to become more mindful of his habit of becoming annoyed, and to try to respond from his values rather than his patterns. He was slowly becoming aware of how his responses to life's frustrations were blocking closeness in his relationships.

"I'm assessing every component and trying to figure out how I can handle things better the next time," Jacob said. "I don't want my children seeing me the way I was over the weekend. I have a lot of challenges. I've been really tested. And I've had some failures. But I'm learning from those failures.

I explained The Six Archetypes (from Chapter 8) to Jacob and asked if he noticed any of them in his behavior.

Again, the archetypes are:

- The Vagabond: The loner who chooses not to make lasting connections.
- The Hunter: The manager who prefers controlling all situations.
- The Prey: The wounded one who lives in constant fear of the Hunter.
- The Adventurer: The achiever who constantly seeks significance.
- The Tourist: The perfectionist who only allows others to see a thin veneer of their real self.
- The Traveler: The resilient one who enjoys new surroundings, ideas, and experiences, withstanding heartaches and hardships through relationship.

He said the first three stood out the most—the Vagabond, the Hunter, and the Prey.

Jacob had a controlled agenda. When things didn't go as planned, he felt hurt and insignificant, and wanted to process his feelings alone. The hurt tapped into old wounds. As a youth, Jacob had been bullied extensively at school. Now, as an adult, he admitted, "When I lose control over a situation, I don't want to deal with it." This caused the cat and mouse cycle of losing control as the Hunter, feeling wounded like the Prey, and needing to escape like the Vagabond. Over that weekend, after the full cycle ran its course twice, he was exhausted and felt like he'd disappointed his family.

"What are you coming away with?" I asked Jacob at the end of his session.

"I need to anticipate a loss of control, identify my feelings, and look for an alternative way of responding," he recognized. He agreed to begin developing flexibility within his frustrating and hurtful moments.

Revisiting the initial trigger at work, Jacob continued, "I need to bend instead of break. I need to be strong enough to make that adjustment. I need to recognize the support I have. If I lose control, I can adapt to it in the best way possible. I can identify alternatives. Roll with it. I can ask myself, 'What can I do?' and then give it a shot."

Building relationships means identifying our patterns, learning to manage our emotions and responses, and setting personal boundaries.

Dr. Brené Brown describes boundaries simply as "What is OK and not OK." For instance, we may feel anger, but boundaries dictate how we express it. If we express it poorly, it can have long-term ramifications in relationships. When backed into a corner, some of us use words to relieve the tension. Jacob tended to use escape instead of confrontation. But there is another way—we can choose to respond differently than we feel. We don't have to say everything that comes to mind.

It's important to learn that not everything we feel needs to be verbalized. Words have consequences. We must control how much we express out loud during the height of intense emotions. Letting words fly during the windstorm can cause further damage. After it passes, we can come back and discuss the problem.

Cycles of behavior tend to repeat themselves in relationships until we intentionally change them. Many of these cycles stem from feelings of worthlessness, insignificance, and powerlessness to correct a problem. When a situation taps into those feelings, we react, causing a breach in relationship. For instance, an event may serve as a trigger; then we feel a sense hurt or fear; and that leads to feeling unloved or unlovable. These emotions can overwhelm us and cause us to isolate, become sarcastic, or emotionally back away. That response can lead to loneliness, and the patterns become further entrenched.

To fully own our response pattern, we have to understand that our triggers usually begin in a sense of unworthiness. But while we understand that intellectually, we have to translate that knowledge into a heartfelt response. We have to change the behavior that keeps us isolated and choose another response. It can start by forgiving, asking for forgiveness, reaching out in faith, and trusting again.

NOTHING CAN TAKE AWAY YOUR VALUE

We can't make ourselves more valuable than we already are. We can only stop contributing, stop loving, and stop trying based on the way our present circumstances make us feel. These feelings can lead to us assuming archetype roles that make us feel disconnected and isolated. That's when we decide it's easier to avoid making lasting connections like The Vagabond; to be controlling like the Hunter; to remain wounded like the Prey; looking for significance to replace true connection like the Adventurer; or perfectionism like the Tourist.

Like pulling our hand away from the flame after lighting a candle, we remove ourselves from situations that might cause pain. We withhold love. We yell. We run and hide. We put up a façade. We stop the flow of connection.

We are likely to relate to each of the archetypes at some point in life. We don't set out to be controlling or wounded, but hurtful events can back us into a corner. Our response patterns cut us off from others.

GETTING UNSTUCK

Best selling author, international speaker, and entrepreneur Valorie Burton shares a small part of her story as well as practical life strategies in her book *Brave Enough to Succeed: 40 Strategies for Getting Unstuck*.[3] The book, she says, was written from the viewpoint of both a coach and "someone who has been stuck—many times—and somehow managed to get unstuck." Although she felt stuck in several areas, including finances, relationships seemed to be her biggest hurdle. "I was stuck in habits I didn't even know were a problem," she writes.

Through counseling, research, and prayer, Burton became aware that she had co-dependent behavior patterns. When she realized they were the holding her back from the kind of life she wanted, she became more intentional. She purposed to understand her triggers and to change the cycle that had kept her stuck.

In the book's introduction, Burton provides an overview of codependent behavior taken from Melanie Beattie's book *Codependent No More.*[2] Codependency is broadly defined as, "dependence on the needs of or control by another."[4] Instead of taking complete responsibility for their actions, codependent people are enmeshed in other people's problems and react to the overflow of emotion they feel. Although their thoughts and actions seem to stem from concern for others, they're really about soothing the inner turmoil that comes from not feeling worthy and loved. As described by Beattie, codependent behavior includes[2]:

- Worrying "sick" about others.
- Trying to help in ways that aren't helpful.
- Saying "yes" but meaning to say "no."
- Strongly persuading others to see his/her point of view.
- Sometimes feeling hurt in an effort to avoid hurting someone else's feelings.
- Not trusting his/her own feelings.
- Believing something that wasn't true and then feeling betrayed.
- Getting even.
- Punishing others with words or behavior.
- Believing he/she is not enough and then living that way.

Burton describes how she moved out of codependent behavioral patterns with a proactive approach. She explains a "bathroom mirror" moment when she realized the power to change was within her control. "I was tired of crying, tired of being disappointed, tired of success in other areas and failure in this one... I was no longer willing to be stuck."[3] She began focusing on developing healthy relationships and then worked on becoming the kind of person that could sustain them.

Burton even changed the way she saw herself. She began to imagine herself as a "healthy and whole" person who engaged in "functional relationships" and then slowly aligned with her vision.[3] From being divorced at 36, to remarrying and becoming a step-mother at 40, and then adopting her own child at 42, Burton's journey took her from hurting, to hoping, to healing others.[1] She became a professional life and executive coach, and earned her master's degree in Positive Psychology from the University of Pennsylvania. Using the resilience training she'd received, she created a credentialed instruction program for new life-coaches known as The Coaching and Positive Psychology (CaPP) Institute.[1]

PURPOSEFULLY CHANGING

There is an alternative to reacting to life's frustrations. It involves working through the pain instead of letting the problem become part of us. It's a choice to break the cycle. We can start by asking ourselves whether we are reacting or responding—if our actions are rooted in a sense of intrinsic value or from feeling vulnerable, worthless, or powerless. Regaining control over our thoughts and actions begins with identifying our triggers. The steps include:

1. First, becoming aware of our feelings. We notice that we feel small, hurt, ashamed, unworthy, or unloved.

2. Next, identifying the original event that produced this trigger.

3. Then, taking responsibility over our thoughts and actions. We learn to respond instead of react, managing the uncomfortable feelings as they arise.

4. Finally, finding safe people with whom we can share our story.

There is power in feeling heard and acknowledged. It gives us space to move forward.

FINDING HOPE THROUGH HEALTHY CONNECTIONS

Balance occurs when we allow emotionally healthy people to see our pain and to give us the support, guidance, and love we need to work through it. Instead of reacting, we can openly explain how a particular situation is impacting us. When we give a voice to the darkness, it lets light in, and then healing can follow.

Next, we work toward healthy relationships. Forming these connections takes time and work. It requires us to be vulnerable and to allow people to see our true selves. And sometimes, we have to intentionally pursue new relationships. Kris Vallotton, Senior Associate Leader from Bethel in Redding, CA, believes the process is about intimacy. "Intimacy," he says, "is, *in to me you see*." It's about letting people in.

The process of forming connections is as intricate as weaving a blanket by hand. Just as the knots are woven one at a time, relationships are built moment by moment. How we respond to another person over time will either build the relationship up or tear it down. For trust to grow, we need to have more positive interactions than negative ones with that person, and to allow them to see us and hear us.

THE SYMPHONY FROM A CONNECTED LIFE

When we connect with others, they hear our song and it becomes part of their symphony. We stop focusing on pain and start living with intentionality. Building connections looks like something. It sounds like something. It's an action. And that action is to move toward relationship instead of avoiding it.

But we can't form these bonds if we're stuck in patterns that prevent them. We can't become vulnerable with people we're trying to control. We can't let ourselves be known to others while trying to manage their perceptions of us. When we hide, and others can't see who we really are, we can't build upon the small experiences necessary to establish trust. We can only connect when we're willing to reveal our imperfections.

We can't manage or control the beauty that comes from allowing ourselves to be known. This means people may see us when we're not perfectly put together. But when we reveal ourselves to others without putting up a front or worrying about getting hurt, we can set aside much of the pretense that causes disconnection. We can talk about what's really going on inside of us.

What might happen if we risk being known? Some people will like us, and some won't. The outcome isn't up to us and can't be controlled. Our job is to simply be open to building a network of people with whom we can share life's ups and downs.

Finding purpose in the midst of pain requires faith that we can bounce back after hardship and move toward relationships with courage. It requires resilience and a willingness to look realistically at the thought patterns that are holding us back. It takes persistence. Most of all, it begins with the knowledge that we are worthy of love.

HERE'S WHAT I WOULD SAY TO TREVOR AND TO YOU

Connecting with others is a choice and an action. Try to understand your patterns for dealing with problems so they don't keep you disconnected. The world around you is waiting for the melody of your song. You are worthy of love and belonging. I encourage you to notice any behaviors that have prevented you from finding the nurturing you need to move forward.

We can't manage or control the beauty that comes from allowing ourselves to be known. This means people may see us when we're not perfectly put together. But when we reveal ourselves to others without putting up a front or worrying about getting hurt, we can set aside much of the pretense that causes disconnection. We can talk about what's really going on inside of us.

Questions for reflection:

1. Do you notice a cycle where you move in and out of various archetype roles? If so, what is your typical reaction pattern?

2. If you were going to operate more like the Traveler, and less like the other archetypes, what is something that would need to shift in you or your behavior?

3. How would you feel about putting a conscious end to the pattern that keeps you isolated?

. . . .

References

1. About Valorie Burton. (n.d.). Retrieved July 2, 2019, from https://valorieburton.com/about/

2. Beattie, M. (1992). Codependent No More; & Beyond Codependency. New York, NY: MJF Books.

3. Burton, V. (2017). Brave Enough to Succeed: 40 Strategies for Getting Unstuck. Harvest House.

4. Codependency. (n.d.). Retrieved July 1, 2019, from https://www.merriam-webster.com/dictionary/codependency

FOURTH LIFE LESSON: CREATE THE LIFE YOU'RE BORN TO HAVE

SITTING AT THE piano, he felt each note deeply, as if his soul could touch the music coming out from under his fingers. His mission was to breathe life into symphonies that would be remembered alongside well-regarded musical icons like Coltrane and Gershwin. He had two loves—music and his family. Music filled him with significance, and family fueled the intensity with love.

Based on a true story, the movie *Mr. Holland's Opus* underscores how sharing the music inside of us can bring out the masterpiece in someone else.[1]

Played by Richard Dreyfuss, who won an Academy Award for his role, Mr. Holland once had a vision for his life—to become a professional, respected composer.[1] Instead, to make a living, he's forced to take a job teaching music at a local high school.

Although initially disgusted with the sound his students make, he eventually comes to realize that the quality of their music is directly tied to his willingness to express his own passion. Beyond teaching them to read music, Mr. Holland begins to infuse them with his love for the art. As he does this, his dreams shift from what he can create on his own to what he can inspire in others.

Many years later, when the school loses its funding for the music program, Mr. Holland is forced into retirement. Joined by his wife and grown son, he takes his last walk through the halls, believing they're headed home—where his dream began—and wondering if his life's work had made a difference.

But instead of leaving the building, his family unexpectedly takes him into the auditorium.[2]

The auditorium is filled with students present and past, all there to honor the man who did more for them than teach music. Every seat is filled and all eyes are on him as he walks the long aisle one last time. He takes a seat at the front of the room alongside his family.

In her speech to honor Mr. Holland, one of his former students, Gertrude Lang, now the state governor, shares sentiments about what a profound influence he's been on her life. She turns directly to him to speak hope and encouragement into his life, just like he had done for her so many years earlier.

"Look around you," she says, her voice beginning to waver. "There is not a life in this room that you have not touched, and each one of us is a better person because of you. We are your symphony, Mr. Holland. We are the melodies and notes of your opus and we are the music of your life."

Because of his willingness to set aside his dream of becoming a famous composer, his passion instead became a priceless personal message, a soul symphony of sorts that impacted many people in his community—including his own family.

I believe this movie portrays what it looks like when we imagine using our talents one way but are confronted with a different reality.

The final section of this book is about realizing the meaning in our own life, aligning our life with our values, and playing our "song," even when the dream happens differently than we expected. It's a process of letting go of what we think life should look like, and sharing our passions and strengths despite the possibility of frustration and rejection. The process includes trying again after failing, despite the opinions of others.

This section demonstrates that there's a season for each of our dreams. Preparation always precedes a plan. In Chapter 10, we explore what these seasons may look like. In Chapter 11, we realize that what prevents us from moving toward a deeply fulfilling life is our focus on fear instead of our reliance on faith. Chapter 12 demonstrates the internal process we undergo before seeing the full manifestation of our dreams.

We can't realize all of our deepest desires overnight. Some may take months or years. We have to recognize the season we're in and simply take the next step forward. Through the journey, we will find that the process of taking those steps changes us. We will almost never see how things will work out in advance. We may even believe our dreams will never materialize. But if we continue to take even the tiniest steps forward, at some point we'll look back and see not only how far we've come, but also what we've achieved and how our melody has become part of our community.

. . . .

References

1. Mr. Holland's Opus (1995). (n.d.). Retrieved November 28, 2017, from http://www.imdb.com/title/tt0113862/

2. Mr. Holland's Opus - Farewell, Mr. Holland. (2009, July 28). Retrieved November 28, 2017, from https://www.youtube.com/watch?v=U8E807R7GkI

CHAPTER TEN

Strategy #10: Recognize the season

‎――――――――――

"It's not hard to make decisions when you
know what your values are."

\- Roy E. Disney

"I WANT TO ask you something," said my friend of more than 20 years. Rebecca almost never asked my opinion about important subjects in her life.

"How can I help?" I asked.

Rebecca was trying to decide whether or not to go back to school for a new career. She was a stay-at-home mother of three, and had little time to herself, as her husband was often out of town on business. But she'd just learned her husband would have the next two years off from traveling, and this would give her a bit more freedom.

"Everyone I've talked to says I should take advantage of the opportunity and go back to school right now."

"What's holding you back?" I asked.

"I don't want to miss anything," she said referring to her family—games, recitals, or time at the park with her kids.

"Is it because of guilt over doing something for you, or is it because you legitimately want to be there for your family?" I asked in hopes of getting to the underlying hesitation in registering for school.

"I thought about that," she said. "It's the latter. I want to be there for my family. I don't want someone else to raise my kids." She wanted to see all of their milestones and attend their events.

Growing up, Rebecca never let anyone see her pain. She put on a happy face and hid behind a "can-do" attitude. She had learned to do this due to a complicated and sometimes painful family history. After her parents separated and her mother remarried, she had been given up for adoption by her birth father, and was later neglected by her adoptive father. She had a tenuous relationship with her mother. She was a freshman in college when she got pregnant with her first child, and put her baby, a little girl, up for adoption. She was in her 20s when she overcame cancer the first time.

Years later, she would finally begin to reveal the pain in her story. Rebecca's top value was family. In her 30s, that value was more apparent than ever. She maintained contact with her eldest child, playing an active role in her life. She dealt with reconciliation before her biological father died and the heartache after his passing. She took steps to build a strong relationship with her mother. After learning her stepfather's life would end prematurely, she took him into her home, supervising his medical treatment plan, bringing him on family excursions, and treating him as if he did not have the illness to which his mind and body were succumbing.

Rebecca spent her life hiding her pain. There were many times when I only found out about her distressing events after the fact, like after she brought her stepfather to live with her and after she finished cancer treatment for the second time. She was good at hiding painful stories and disconnecting from others while she was in the middle of processing trauma.

Now, years later, I was becoming aware of an overarching theme in Rebecca's life. Despite her pain, there was a tapestry of relationships she had intentionally mended and woven together. It became clear the afternoon I had called to catch up. She revealed that her grandmother had passed away earlier that week—again, not telling me until her initial shock had subsided.

Her story of reconciliation and overcoming cancer made her caretaking role not just something she did, but a part of her larger purpose. She wanted to be present in her children's lives and was struggling with the idea of putting someone else in charge while she went to school.

"Values," I explained to Rebecca, "are something you model your actions and your life around. They're the things that matter most to you. If you don't have points of action around them, they aren't values—they're ideals. From what I hear you saying, your family is your top value."

I explained that for many mothers, staying home with their kids isn't a high priority. If it was to Rebecca, no one should tell her otherwise.

Over the course of her life, Rebecca really had lived out of her highest value—maintaining a strong family bond. Despite the personal cost, she had reconnected with her mother, re-established a relationship with her birth father, cared for her sick stepfather, learned how to home school her son and preschool daughter while playing with her toddler, made meals from scratch, and kept her home immaculate. She had become the kind of person who prepared homemade bone soup, created elaborate hair ribbons and birthday parties to delight her small daughter, and breast-fed her babies for two years each. (With three children at home, that meant six total years of breastfeeding.)

She had sacrificed herself personally in every possible way.

She had also put the pursuit of her own career on hold while helping her husband achieve his vision. She had assisted him with his schoolwork when he went back to college. She had packed up her entire home to move each time his job took them to a new location—sometimes to a different country. To help give him the rest he needed, she stayed up nights when their kids were sick, and still managed to lead a support group for women whose husbands also traveled for living.

Rebecca was excited about pursuing her dream career. Although her other friends were encouraging her to do it, I heard her telling me a different story. From my perspective, she was saying that she was already doing what she valued most. Her professional goals would be realized in a different season of life than she had initially envisioned.

It wasn't that she'd never have a career; it was about deciding what was best for her right now. The big vision would eventually include school and a career. Postponing school didn't make it less important. It simply meant she had a different priority for the season she was in.

Rather than basing her decision about school on her husband's more flexible schedule, I wanted her to make the decision based on what mattered most to her right now. If her choice was based on passion for a job and serving others, and she was OK with having outside help at home—then she should go back to school. But if her highest, current value was to continue caring for her family while her children were still young, then she should do that.

"Listen to the small voice inside," I mentioned to her at the close of our conversation, "and not the one that roars."

Like I explained to Rebecca that day, an ideal is something you regard as perfect and aim for—as in, "in an ideal world, this is the way it would be done." According to the Google definition of the word, "values" set the standard for actions that we will eventually take.[2] Values, if not set intentionally, will be determined by our lifestyle. We can't say we value something and then not make it a priority. If our values aren't goals we'll eventually make plans to accomplish, then they're not what we value most. They're what we would do under perfect circumstances.

To pursue life-giving decisions, we must determine if our actions are supporting what we say we value most. However, we must also determine if it is the right season for a certain part of our dream to come to life. For instance, Rebecca mentioned two values—attending school to pursue her dream job; and being the primary caretaker for her children. But she couldn't do both full-time. She would have to determine the right order. Keeping her career dreams alive didn't necessarily mean she needed to pursue the degree right away—it could be as simple as planning for school and starting with the prerequisites.

One year after our conversation, Rebecca signed up to take a pre-requisite college course. Her career was a few years away, but she had taken one step in the right direction.

> Listen to the small voice inside, and not the one that roars.

THREE KEYS TO CHECKING THE SEASON

Big dreams happen in stages and in the right seasons of life. We can shelve a dream, knowing that while we will eventually move toward it, we can put other goals first and still be living out of our values. Other times, we can work toward dreams—even when other people have determined for us that it's not the right season. The order in which we pursue our goals does not dictate their level of importance. Just because we don't reap the full reward in the immediate future does not mean that it isn't on the way.

When we make plans to pursue what we value most, we are living congruently. Some seasons are for planning, other seasons are for taking action. When we don't move toward our dreams, we have to ask ourselves, "What is holding us back?" Are we sacrificing our dreams for the safety of living a small life, or are we choosing to prioritize a different path? Living congruently means we show up to "play," aligning our life with plans for what we value most. Then during the right seasons, when specific dreams should be birthed, we move toward them.

In moving forward, we need to ask ourselves three things:

1. Are we acting out of our highest values? Meaning, we need to ask ourselves if this goal we have created is congruent with what we value most.

2. Is this the season for that dream to come to life? If this goal is not a priority yet, we need to identify our priority for the season we are in. Here's a hint: We will usually have some sort of desire to accomplish that dream.

3. Are we using excuses or blame to avoid facing fear? For instance, when we are presented with the opportunity to follow our dreams, we may shift our focus to excuses. Excuses can really be intentional roadblocks we create to avoid feeling powerless about the outcome. When we are able to blame someone or something else, we don't have to face the under-lying anxiety that accompanies uncertainty about the future.

ALIGNING WITH OUR HIGHEST VALUE

Three years after joining Canada's *Second City Television* (*SCTV*), at age 30, Rick Moranis wrote, directed and starred in his first film, *Strange Brews*. Released in 1983, the film was a collaboration with *SCTV* co-star Dave Thomas, based on their *Second City* characters— stereotypical Canadian brothers who find themselves in terrible but funny situations.[3]

After *Strange Brews*, Moranis' film career soared. Over the next few years, he won back-to-back starring roles in more than 15 films, working with comedy legends such as Steve Martin, Bill Murray, and Dan Aykroyd. Highlights include *Ghostbusters* (1984), *Little Shop of*

Horrors (1986), *Spaceballs* (1987), *Ghostbusters II* (1989), *Parenthood* (1989), and *Honey, I Shrunk the Kids* (1989).[4]

His next triumph was in 1991, when he landed the lead role of "Phil" in the film *City Slickers*. But that same year, Moranis' wife, Anne Belsky, was diagnosed with breast cancer. Moranis pulled out of *City Slickers* to care for her and their children. Belsky died later that year.[3]

In the six years following his wife's untimely death, Moranis continued making movies, but found it increasingly difficult to juggle his career with his other lead role—single father. Raising his children was his highest priority, and his film career required being away from home for extended periods of time. So at the height of his career, 44-year-old Moranis stepped away from stardom to be a stay-at-home dad.[3]

Moranis says he didn't labor over the decision. He wanted his kids to have the kind of wholesome upbringing that he'd enjoyed. So he aligned his actions with his highest value. He continued working, but focused on roles that allowed him to stay in town, such as voice-over and TV roles.[5]

In a rare interview on the podcast "Bullseye with Jesse Thorn," Moranis describes his choice: "I applied all of my creativity to my home life, to my kids, to my family. I was the same person. I didn't change. I just shifted my focus. When my kids came home, there was music, and there were lights on, and there were great smells coming out of the kitchen. It was just a joyful place to be, and that's what I wanted."[5]

THE NEXT RIGHT STEP

Most of the time, we can't see how things will come together. But if we keep moving toward our vision, living our highest values, and setting goals, it will come together. We're each at different phases of moving toward dreams, and letting others go dormant for a certain season.

Sometimes we can feel very removed from the kind of life we would like to live. The big vision may feel so distant that we can hardly imagine what our life would look like if things were to finally change. It can be a huge act of faith to take the tiniest step toward a big goal or our vision for our future self. It can also feel like a massive act of courage to wait to pursue some of our big dreams. We have to persist past the fear that invites us into a belief that because we aren't taking action toward a big dream that we will never accomplish it. Sometimes our best, next step is to make the smallest of preparations for a future goal. In the meantime, we must align our life with our deepest values even before the big dream comes.

Part of the process is finding comfort in the season we're in. It means we continue to show up even when are in the middle of what may feel like a detour. Only after we layer in the texture of time, people, and achievements do we hear the symphony, and see the results of a life that has been consistently aligned with value and purpose.

HERE'S WHAT I WOULD SAY TO TREVOR AND TO YOU

Like I told Rebecca that day, "Listen to the small voice inside, and not the one that roars." A certain problem might be roaring right now, saying you will never find peace or overcome that obstacle; choose to listen to a different voice. Listen to the one that whispers hope; the same one that encourages you to live out of your values. All things are possible but not all things are good in every season. Don't be deflated if it takes a while to move toward your big dreams. Good things take time.

Even if it isn't the right season to move forward, plan anyway. Live out of your values and don't worry about how things will all come together. Continue to do things that inspire you while consistently taking small steps in the right direction. Don't compare yourself to others along the way; stay focused on your purpose and your strengths. If you keep moving toward your big vision, even if it's only one small step at a time, it's enough. You are enough. Stay heartened during the slow seasons. If you do this, things will eventually all come together.

Questions for reflection:

1. What are your values; i.e. what do you value most in your life?

2. Are you truly aligning your internal thoughts, conversations with others, actions, and schedule with your highest values?

3. Are you trying to achieve something that might be better accomplished in a different season of life?

. . . .

References

1. Definition of ideal. (n.d.). Retrieved November 28, 2017, from http://www.dictionary.com/browse/ideals

2. Definition of values. (n.d.). Retrieved November 28, 2017, from http://www.dictionary.com/browse/values

3. Raga, S. (2018, May 08). 12 Fascinating Facts About Rick Moranis. Retrieved July 1, 2019, from http://mentalfloss.com/article/77439/12-facts-about-rick-moranis

4. Rick Moranis. (n.d.). Retrieved from https://www.imdb.com/name/nm0001548/

5. Rowles, D. (2019, March 12). Rick Moranis Opens Up About Retiring From Acting To Be A Stay-At-Home Dad In Rare Interview. Retrieved July 1, 2019, from https://uproxx.com/tv/rick-moranis-the-best-celebrity-dad-of-all-time-opens-up-about-his-retirement-from-acting/

CHAPTER ELEVEN

STRATEGY #11:
RELEASE THE EXCUSES AND
STEP OUT IN FAITH

"A man cannot be comfortable without his own approval."

– Mark Twain

"I HAVE A vision of who I know I can be, but sometimes I put excuses in my path, or tell myself, 'I can't be that,'" said my new coaching client, Amber.

Amber disliked her current job. She wanted to open her own boot camp fitness program. But feelings of low self-worth kept her from moving forward.

And something even worse held her back—a past, perceived failure. She'd opened a small workout studio previously, and later had to close it.

"It's a battle with myself," Amber confided. "I know what I want, but I can't picture going after it again." Her vision was blocked by several things—fear, a sense of disempowerment, and too much concern about what other people think. She doubted her qualifications, so she felt like she'd fail. But if she did succeed, she feared she'd be unable to live up to people's expectations or that she'd be thought of as a fraud.

Amber's actual life experiences included success. She'd helped many people as a coach and personal trainer, and felt like she had the tools to develop her own program. But she was scared to do so, because it might fail. In her mind, failing twice would make *her* a failure. She would need a major degree of faith to take another chance.

"I'm wondering how you would feel if you tried again in spite of the fear," I mused.

"There is already so much out there in the fitness world," she replied, still focused on the details. "Can I set the fear and criticism aside, and know that what I am doing is making a difference? I want to help people, but I don't know if I can."

"What I hear you saying is, 'Can I rise above the critics?'" I responded.

Completely in flow, she interjected, "I know I'm going to fail along the way. I've already had a little studio for a year and I had to close it. I'm in a small town. I need to step outside of caring what others think," she said, "I know I need to overcome that."

While she was concerned about other people's opinions, I had a different focus. "I'm curious what *you* think," I said. "How do you feel about your future despite closing the studio?"

"That it's all I'm going to do." She was referring to failing. She was sure that her past failure meant she was doomed to fail again.

Amber was deeply moved at her own revelation.

"I struggle with that question every day," she said. "Sometimes I feel as long as I'm moving toward my goal, even with small steps, I'm succeeding. In other ways, I feel like I'm not doing enough, or I don't know how to do more."

"What if you believed you had the right tools to do what you are supposed to do right now?" I asked in hopes she would break her out of her circular thinking.

"I'd probably see things a lot more clearly and from a different perspective," she said. "I would also move forward differently."

"And what if you didn't fail?" I asked.

"I don't look at that side often enough," said Amber.

She audibly exhaled, as though the weight she'd been carrying came out in one big sigh.

In our session, Amber had listed many excuses for feeling stuck: worry about the future; the insecurity of failing again; concern about what others think; and the fear of trying again—and possibly succeeding.

"So what is the right answer for you?" I asked.

"I've got to make a plan?" Realizing she asked it as a question, she laughed. I could hear hope starting to rise in the inflection and cadence of her voice.

Many of us stop for fear of what might happen next. We've failed before and do our best to avoid failing again. We can't see the beginning for the end, or how things will come together, so we don't even try. Fear of the unknown can cause us to back away from the things we are most passionate about.

Like I told Amber that day, when we are wading toward our purpose in life, we've got to wade through the fear. Many of us sit on the side of the pool feeling like we've missed out because of past mistakes, and because of what people have said or might say, and from our feelings of unworthiness. *Moving through our fear means taking the next step, even though we don't know how everything will turn out. It is a step of faith.*

THE ANSWERS ARRIVE IN TIME

After working on a major project, my husband and I were confronted with a seemingly impossible situation. For two months, we'd devoted ourselves full time to selling products for a particular business, and at the end of it, the owner didn't pay us. He left us with a substantial debt during a particularly vulnerable time for us. I was pregnant, and Ken's traveling had slowed down, reducing our income.

We were left with more questions than answers: Why did the owner do this to us? How would we pay off the debt? Where would we find the income we needed to sustain us until Ken's work started picking back up?

My heart was bitter toward this man for the way he had used us, stolen our time and products, and then lied about us to others. I felt hurt, overwhelmed and frustrated. We went into survival mode for the next year. We weren't sure if we ever wanted to work with another business partner again. We sought business law advice, to no avail.

There was nothing we could do. Maligning him was against our character. Pursuing a lawsuit would be more costly than what he owed us, and there was no guarantee we'd win.

I just couldn't get past the shock of betrayal.

However, the first step in moving forward was forgiving the person who had wronged us. It didn't mean the debt he left us with would vanish, but it did mean we could release the emotional heaviness and bitterness. Forgiveness freed up the emotional space to resurrect old dreams and allowed us to move ourselves out of the financial hole.

In survival mode, I remember taking inventory of what I had to sell. My mind first wandered to household items. Then I remembered the library of training videos Ken and I had produced a couple of years earlier. At one time I had thought we would partner with a large company to distribute them. However, each time we approached the target company, they declined the opportunity for partnership. We wondered if the library would ever pay for itself.

After our baby arrived, pressed for a way to pay the debt we still owed, I asked Ken to reach out to that company one last time. Miraculously, this time, we got a different response. They went on to tell us that they now had the technology to partner with us.

Apparently they had sent us an email sometime back to explore partnership possibilities. Due to exhaustion, we had missed the emails.

We went on to work out a partnership to sell two full courses.

Before the courses went live, there were a few months of extra work, more business expenses, and a big blank space of time where we were left to wonder if we might be setting ourselves up to fail again. Trying again could mean failing again. We were still paying the price of the first failure, and we also had a video collection that had sold modestly well on our platform, but never really had taken off like we once dreamed. It almost seemed silly to hope again.

Despite our past failure, we did hope again. Waiting during the holidays before our courses went live was uncomfortable. There was no guarantee that our new partnership would work or that our courses would sell.

Taking that next step was taking a risk. We might not succeed, and we risked looking bad to our industry peers. We took the next steps anyway. Then we waited.

STARTING WITH SEEDS

Very often, the beginnings of our biggest dreams don't come wrapped in the packages we have envisioned. Most of us would like to have all the details worked out in advance so as to take the next right step. We would like to know that our actions will lead to success. Many of us want to see the fruit before we plant the tree. But our dreams don't always come true in the prescribed order we'd like.

During the time before the courses launched, Ken and I had questions and apprehension about how it would work out. We would never have experienced the series of unexpected answers had we refused to try. The answers only showed up as we took the next step in our journey.

DO IT AFRAID

Here's the key: We have to take that next step before we have worked the details out. We know the objective, but the way forward is full of obstacles. We have to take each day, moment by moment.

If our goal is a priority, we need to overcome our excuses so that we can pursue it. This may mean moving forward afraid and full of apprehension. In a business, or a relationship, it means trying again and possibly failing again.

We need to ask ourselves, "If I wasn't afraid to take the next step, what would I do?" The answer to that question is the answer for how to move forward. Most of us would love to see the big vision before we take the next step. Like Indiana Jones crossing the bridge, we would be very comforted by seeing the bridge and not just having conceptual knowledge that it existed. But very often the next, faith-filled step is central to moving forward and expressing our life's melody. Faith comes in knowing the bridge will be there to meet us as we step out.

LIVING IN THE TENSION OF A NEW STORY

The thing that keeps us stuck is telling ourselves a story with a preconceived ending. If we're not moving toward our dreams, that story might be standing in the way of our future success. We may be telling ourselves that we're:

- Not equipped for the journey
- We don't have the _____ we need
- Too old
- Too young
- We'll fail if we try
- We aren't smart enough
- We aren't successful enough
- We are a fraud

The list is endless. If we act on fear instead of faith, we will stay small. Fear will keep us from showing up and trying. Fear will always cause our melody to weaken, grow dull, and eventually fade until it drains our self worth and we begin to believe our melody isn't worth playing. Living in the tension means we move forward in faith despite the questions about how it will all work out.

EACH OF US IS UNIQUE

Each of us has something inside that is a special combination that only we possess. It is a unique expression of ideas, thoughts, passions, credentials, experiences, kindness, love, and zeal. If these attributes have been diminished, it's time to practice using what we have. We may have to start small. We may even have to remind ourselves of that dream we once had many years ago. It's OK if we've forgotten, but it's time to remember. If we could move fear aside, what would we hope for once more? Remember the passions. Remember the goals. Remember who we once were before we stopped putting our melody "out there" for others to hear.

Next year, let's not be where we are today. Let's move into the new. Let's step into something we've always dreamed about.

Amber wanted to start her own program. Fear and not knowing how things would work out were initially preventing her from taking the next big step. Months after our coaching sessions, Amber did wind up teaching her own boot camp program. I've since enjoyed reading her social media posts about her clients' weight loss journey successes. Amber's breakthrough paved the way for other people to experience breakthrough. Just like she took the next, best step forward, each of us can take one little step toward what we desire most without having all of the details worked out in advance.

Beyond goals, we have to ask ourselves what our heart most deeply desires. Put differently, if given the opportunity, what would we really like to do, see, or attract into our lives? Perhaps we would like to be business owners. Maybe a change of careers is in order or even a subtle shift in responsibilities. Developing close relationships or working toward better health might be the most important thing right now. Whatever it is, we need to go for it with our whole heart. When we choose to move forward despite the fear, our life becomes a light to others. Our pain will become part of our purpose. Everything that kept us small will cause us to shine. When we shine, we radiate hope to people who need our light. This becomes our melody.

Let me be clear: When we allow our light to shine and our melody to be heard, despite our fear and insecurities, people we were meant to impact will forever be changed, inspired, and encouraged to let *their* light shine and to let *their* melody be heard. It all starts with the belief that we can still make a difference and that there is something worthwhile in us to be passed along to others.

HERE'S WHAT I WOULD SAY TO TREVOR AND TO YOU

When you begin to accept your own worthiness, you can create a picture in your mind's eye of how you would like to pursue your dreams and passions. It's at that point that you can effectively create and move toward your goals. You may have to move forward with limited information. You may have to do it in spite of your fear.

Your biggest successes will nearly always start as small seeds with stories of failure that will happen along the way. You might not realize it right now, but your experiences have helped build your skills that will set you up for future success. If used the

> When we choose to move forward despite the fear, our life becomes a light to others. Our pain will become part of our purpose. Everything that kept us small will cause us to shine. When we shine, we radiate hope to people who need our light. This becomes our melody.

right way, all of your life experiences can come together to help you—even the things that you might not be proud of or things that don't seem exciting. How you think about your past experiences—even your failures—where you came from, what you are capable of, and who you are, will determine how far you will go.

Don't let worry about the unknown parts of the future hold you back from the steps you know you need to take today. You were created to live a bold life. Think big. Now take one step in the right direction. You can do this!

Questions for reflection:

1. Are you using excuses or blame to avoid facing fear?

2. When you're presented with the opportunity to follow your dreams, do you shift your focus to excuses?

3. If you weren't afraid to take the next right step, what would you do?

CHAPTER TWELVE

STRATEGY #12:
RISE FROM PAIN TO PURPOSE

—————

"If you go to work on your goals, your goals will go to work on you. If you go to work on your plan, your plan will go to work on you. Whatever good things we build end up building us."

— Jim Rohn

WHEN SHE FIRST approached me for coaching, Kylie wanted to work on three major life changes: exploring the ramifications of having another child, developing a business and ministry while maintaining a current income, and finding a feeling of fulfillment while prioritizing her personal relationships.

She was a working mom in her 40's with two children—one from a previous marriage and another from her current marriage. She wanted to become pregnant with a third child, and she knew that at her age, time was of the essence.

She had two jobs—a part-time position where she wasn't happy, and her own personal training and group exercise business, which was floundering.

While Kylie had a good life, she was afraid her dreams would never see the light of day. She wanted to be 400 steps farther down the path, but she couldn't figure out which single step she should take next. She felt like she was grieving over what could have been, and what had not yet happened. "I don't have a roadmap yet," she said. "I'm waiting for the right doors to open."

Kylie believed the key to success was to write down her goals and move toward them. And while that's a good practice, for her, there would be more to it. Realizing her dreams would require an accompanying personal inner process. The path couldn't be perfectly clear and finalized now. Each of her aspirations would have its season. Some would happen quickly, but other goals would take more time.

The first season of Kylie's evolution had to include an emotional transformation. She needed to develop the skills necessary for her path: discipline, strength, commitment, and perseverance. Taking the next step before she was ready could be futile. She needed to become someone who could sustain her accomplishments. Her first steps would need to be small and character-shaping.

Realizing adoption was their best chance for another child, Kylie's husband pressed her to explore the possibility. But Kylie wasn't sure she wanted to do it. She wrote to me between sessions: "When we first discussed it, it made sense. Today, I'm not so sure. Adoption will be a long process. I'm not ready right now." As if to add emphasis to her indecision, she humorously added, "Oh, and I'd like a Boxer puppy."

A month after our first session, she wrote me an update—not about adoption, but about her business. "I'm closing my fitness business. One day, I'll start it over. Right now, I figure I'll just lay here and molt, and embrace the desk with my head face-down in a pool of tears." She was in the thick of the process.

Weeks later, we re-approached the subject of adoption. I began our session by asking, "How have you been feeling about it?" She was still unsure, but despite her turmoil, Kylie finally agreed to adopt through the foster care system.

She continued working at her part-time job while looking for a new one. She didn't realize it at the time, but her life, dreams, and endeavors were all in flux—and moving forward in indefinable increments. The process was like being sandpapered: What would eventually make her polished would be uncomfortable while it was happening. She noticed herself changing inside. She was about to undergo a deep emotional metamorphosis.

"I think I need to release the illusion of control," she said.

Yet she still worried about things beyond her control, like how she and her husband would manage with another child and why her fitness business hadn't flourished.

It had been seven months since our first conversation. Looking back at our sessions, I asked, "Where were you, emotionally?"

"In a whirlwind—a dust storm," she said. "I needed to get it out."

"Where are you now?" I asked.

"Still dusty. I still have a taste of chalk in my mouth. I'm nervous about life transitions." She pointed out that she was still filling out adoption paperwork, looking for a new job, and trying to plan a new fitness business.

"I've been in a funk," she continued. "Restless. I've been battling myself more than anything." She was frustrated with her lack of progress and grieving for the life she thought she would have had by then. "I want this to be that 'now time,'" she said.

Kylie and her husband had completed the initial foster/adopt process and had begun fostering children. But it wasn't going as she had envisioned it. Each of the children was either returned to its birth parents or adopted by a family who had priority on the waiting list. Losing these children was heartbreaking for her, because she became attached to each one. She was in the middle of a long season of much labor but no fruit, and she was beginning to wonder if things would ever turn around.

But she kept pressing forward. That was fortunate, because her breakthrough was right around the corner. It would be an outgrowth of her internal changes—her learning to deal with the discomfort and uncertainty of not having the new job, the thriving business, or the baby, for an extended period.

DORMANT DREAMS ARE NOT DEAD

Some of us have dreams we thought were dead. But they weren't—they were only dormant. It's time to revisit them. We need to remember we want to help change the world and leave a legacy.

When my husband and I lived in the Bay Area in California, we had a small garden in the front of our home. I had bought a little tree and put it in a planter next to the front door. Since we were on the West Coast, the weather was pretty consistent from season to season, so a couple of times a week, all year round, I would stand outside and water the garden.

One day while I was watering, I realized my tree had died. The only problem was that I wasn't sure how to dispose of it. So, instead of throwing it out—and partly out of pity—I continued to water it along with the other plants. Although I thought it was a lost cause, I stood outside and watered it twice a week.

Months later, I noticed something. Buds were starting to form on the dead-looking branches. The tree hadn't died. It had been dormant.

I later realized it was a perfect metaphor for the process that we endure throughout different seasons of our lives.

BLOOMING

When we first started, Kylie equated many of her dreams to being a dead tree. But they weren't dead. They were dormant.

About a year and a half after we first started coaching together, Kylie saw incredible changes. They didn't happen all at once, but she secured a new job, finalized the adoption of a baby girl she'd taken care of since birth, and had restarted her fitness business.

When she first approached me for coaching around the subjects of having another child, developing a business and ministry, her work, and finding a feeling of fulfillment while prioritizing her personal relationships—she had no way of knowing her vision would eventually come to fruition—but differently than she expected. She didn't realize she would first need to go through a process that would clarify her priorities, solidifying the foundation from which she would grow.

STEPS TOWARD REALIZING THE DREAM

Dreams often come to fruition after a long period of dormancy. Something good is about to bud, but it won't bloom out of season. Dreams may look dead, but it doesn't mean they are dead. Different dreams come to fruition at different points. Like Kylie, we may be reaping the harvest in relationship, but feel stifled in our job or in her case, in ministry.

During the wait, we are developing important skills. We will eventually realize the dream if we continue taking baby steps toward it. Dreams can take many years to fully manifest. During our dormant season we can do five things:

1. Realign with the belief that we are enough, right here, right now, in the midst of the seemingly unfruitful season.

2. Seek inner healing in the deep areas that cause us to feel like we are not enough, not loved, and not seen.

3. Become mindful of behavior that keeps us feeling unfulfilled, isolated, and discouraged.

4. Live congruently with the tenets of our faith, life's purpose, or highest intentions.

5. Discover our deepest values and align our actions/choices with those sacred core truths.

The fruit of our labor will eventually yield a harvest. None of our efforts are wasted. We are in the midst of a flourishing success story. Although we may think we need to do more, earn more, or accumulate one more thing, we are enough just as we are. Overcoming fear, recognizing our own value, telling our stories, and letting love in is how we continue to change and flourish.

THE DREAM IS STILL POSSIBLE

Believing that we can achieve our dreams is the first step in achieving them. We can start thinking outside of the box and using our creativity to imagine a better life. While we may not have control over the obstacles that arise, we are in control of our lives. Our past does not have to define our future. More importantly, our life's events do not determine our worthiness. Feeling worthy is a choice, despite what past circumstances might have us believe. It's a choice to embrace a powerful, hope-filled new message.

What might change in our lives if we took complete control over the story we've been telling ourselves? Could we allow the process to happen without hopelessness and resistance?

The interesting thing about developing a vision and big goals for our lives is that they rarely manifest like we had planned. Sometimes our big dream seems impossible. But we have to stay focused on it while building relationships. The steps are rarely clearly defined, but like Indiana Jones' first step forward, the bridge will be there to meet us. It may unfold differently than we originally imagined. There may be points where our dream goes dormant and the progress becomes about our process.

During the process, the biggest points of learning tend to be around our own resilience, perseverance, and developing the kind of character that can then serve others who are currently in similar situations. Clarity comes with perspective. Perspective requires two key ingredients—time and patience. We must acknowledge our positive steps in the right direction.

One obstacle toward forward motion is focusing on how we failed—the detour that derailed us from the life we desired. It's natural to grieve our aborted dreams, for a time. But staying locked in that grief can keep hope at bay.

Here are a few keys for the journey:

- We can only achieve our true purpose when we begin walking toward it

- We will find our next step by dreaming about it first

- We can only experience deeply fulfilling relationships when we risk being known

We can only start dreaming again if we're willing to move forward despite how we feel right now. We'll never see the twists and turns in the path in advance. But we'll know the next right step intuitively. We have to listen to the small voice inside. The key is to take the step toward what we want in this season of life and deal with the obstacles as they arise, instead of stopping due to fear of the unknown. We'll never appreciate what we could have done if we don't commit to doing it.

The pages of this book reveal a process for helping you recognize the path to personal reinvention. The chapters outline the need to:

1. Construct a fresh core belief.

2. Lose the scarcity mindset.

3. Rewrite the story.

While we may not have control over the obstacles that arise, we are in control of our lives. Our past does not have to define our future. More importantly, our life's events do not determine our worthiness. Feeling worthy is a choice, despite what past circumstances might have us believe. It's a choice to embrace a powerful, hope-filled new message.

4. Recognize the third solution.

5. Avoid counterproductive thinking and habits.

6. Change the inner voice.

7. Let it go.

8. Let love in.

9. Learn the art of connection.

10. Recognize the season.

11. Release the excuses and step out in faith.

12. Rise from pain to purpose.

This book started by identifying how we get stuck in self-limiting patterns. It doesn't mean that we will never experience those patterns again. It simply means we'll recognize them sooner so that we can break the cycle.

We learned that life is not a series of either/or questions. It is not about a pass/fail outcome. Very often, there is a third solution, even in the midst of dealing with painful problems.

Changing how we think also means changing what we choose to say and do. In order to truly move forward, we have to be willing to stop self-defeating thoughts as they come, change the stories that we allow to repeat in our mind, and break out of self-limiting behavior. We have to limit negative self-talk.

Next, we were challenged with the idea of widening our circle and moving toward relationships. This idea means we have to be willing to let things go and forgive the people who wronged us—focusing on the 98 percent of the people in our lives who matter. Cultivating relationships also means noticing and stepping out of cycles that prevent us from connecting and being loved. We have to learn to develop consistency in all parts of life—including how we show up in relationships.

To cap off the process, we bring the story full circle. We've been challenged to revive the big dream inside of us and looked for where we've held on to excuses or blame in moving toward it. We evaluated whether we are living out of our values and aligning our lives with what is most important for today. Finally, we were challenged to take the next right step forward. It may not turn out the way we expected, but the process will produce the kind of character we need to continue the journey.

OTHERS ARE WAITING FOR YOUR MELODY

When one of our songs is lost, it impacts the greater whole. Can we really imagine life without the contributions from various people such as Steven Spielberg, Confucius, Steve Jobs, and Martin Luther King? How about Mother Teresa, the Dalai Lama, Rosa Parks or Cesar Chavez?

Do we really think that Mother Theresa didn't get tired or ever feel like quitting? Seriously? How we choose to return to a place of hope has massive consequences for not only ourselves but also the world around us.

What if my mentor had been too busy at work to show kindness and support when I needed it most? No, his name won't go down in the history books, but to me, during my time of need, his actions were invaluable. Each of us carries that same type of promise. Really. The people we read about didn't get a magic gene that turned off self-doubt and insecurity. They persisted despite those feelings.

Trevor ended his life because he couldn't see past the temporary acute pain, and as a result, his song ended in his death. I'm certain that Trevor carried the compassion in him that could have changed at LEAST one life. That is what prompted the book—the impact of his lost melody on the world. The domino effect of him playing his song would be an unending legacy. Although they might not remember his song particularly, they would remember the one that was initially influenced by HIM.

In order to play our melody, we must get past the fear and feelings of unworthiness. We are enough. We are loved. We will have no way of knowing that our melody will be just the inspiration and hope that someone else needs to keep playing. We can't always know the fruit of our actions before we take them.

We are all interconnected. Each of our melodies matter—no matter how small they seem or how insignificant we feel. We never know how our lives will touch others. Trevor's life touched mine—and his death led me to write this book—which in turn may inspire someone who reads the pages to sing their song.

That's really what this message is about. To me, this is where the choice to play our song either is born or dies. We must rise above the fear that comes with consistently showing up to play even when we're still in emotional pain, struggling to feel accepted, or believing we're at a dead end.

We can't give up because the dream hasn't come to fruition yet or we don't know how things will turn out. We can't stop because we are still living with self-doubt and condemnation. We must take the next faith-filled step. We can almost never see the end for the beginning.

Winston Churchill once said, "Success is not final, failure is not fatal, it is the courage to continue that counts." We must take heart and keep pressing through the temporary setbacks. We will never know what we can accomplish if we quit trying.

Our song matters. We matter. Each time we take a step, it matters. So let's do what it is we do best, and do it with all of our heart.

We need to remember we are worthy no matter how we feel, what happened to us, or what we've done. We are worthy and worthwhile. We are powerful people with powerful decisions to make. We are lovable despite how we sometimes feel about ourselves and despite our intense desire to self protect. Our current problem is solvable. It will require patience and a creative new thought to solve the old problem. We will feel uncomfortable as we shift out of the old cycles of behavior and allow ourselves to be fully known.

When we are standing in the middle of pain and self-doubt, it's hard to understand that life will not stay as it is. It will be what we make it. If we believe we will never see success, we will stop dreaming. If we believe we can't trust others, we won't take a vulnerable step toward relationship.

It all starts with a belief. What we believe has a direct impact on how we feel about ourselves. Unless we intentionally set out to change, how we feel will impact how far we go in pursuit of our dreams and relationships. Going through the uncomfortable process of change is an important part of moving forward. We become the person who can sustain the dream. In pursuing our dreams, our song comes to life. As we play our song, our melody intertwines with other people's melodies and our collective songs become a symphony. These melodies carry a resonance that will live on as our legacy long after we are gone.

HERE'S WHAT I WOULD SAY TO TREVOR AND TO YOU

Make plans for tomorrow. Get a vision for what you would like your life to be like. Know that it will take time for you to manifest that vision, and don't lose hope. Like my mom has always said to me, "Things have a way of working out." Sometimes they just take a little longer than you expected. Find contentment with where you are today. Place a priority in developing a strong support network so that you have people who will help lift you up when things seem to be going off course—and they probably will from time to time.

Remind yourself about the big dreams you've forgotten or thought were dead. If you've never had big dreams, write down new goals. Begin to foster hope and belief that your dream will one day come into its season and blossom.

Don't give up. Take the next step and don't worry about how it will all come together. We can have the best plans, but sometimes we just have to settle in for the process. If you'll keep going, you will eventually be able to see how the pieces do come together to work in your favor.

Questions for reflection:

1. Are you grieving about something that hasn't happened or something that happened a long time ago?

2. How would it feel to move on from the grief?

3. What would you really like in this next season of your life? What steps are you taking to make this a possibility?

EPILOGUE

I'VE ASKED MYSELF if this book truly contains everything I would have said to my friend Trevor. Or is it only one part of a series of resources that could be used to restore health, happiness, contentment, joy, purpose, and love.

There are brilliant minds like the people who have written and produced the certifications I've taken, like Dr. Brené Brown, Tony Robbins and Cloe Madanes, and Valorie Burton. Dr. Brown has spent her entire career researching, writing, and teaching about vulnerability, courage, and living wholeheartedly. Coaches like Tony Robbins travel the world using methods of strategic intervention to help audience members get out of a rut and move toward the kind of life they believe is possible. Coaches like Valorie Burton speak at conferences for the military and on television using positive psychology to help equip audiences all over the world to live, lead, speak, and act with courage and confidence.

There are way too many resources to list here. Besides well-known authors and speakers, there are also unsung hometown heroes who help from their offices, and even from their phones while sitting in their living rooms, across the world. In writing this book, I've found that the answer comes from the symphony of professionals, mentors, creatives, parents, and friends who play their particular songs to the best of their ability.

So no, it's probably not everything I would have said, but it's enough. Just like the fruit of all of our labor is enough. It's not meant to answer all of the problems. Each of us is only uniquely equipped with a small piece of the overall answer. This book represents a portion of my contribution. Is my song THE answer? No. It is part of the answer.

The rest of the answer is in you.

ACKNOWLEDGEMENTS

WITHOUT MY HUSBAND'S encouragement this book probably would never have seen the light of day. His words of affirmation were a huge reason why I became certified in life coaching in the first place and why I finally finished the book.

Special thanks to my mom, who patiently listens to all of my big ideas and proofread this book over her summer vacation.

Thanks to my editor, coach, and book advocate, Julie Zeitlin. If my book reads well, it's because of her. I'd also like to acknowledge Sally Schloss, my second book editor. Her humor and passion is contagious. Additionally, I appreciate Eric Poppen for the final edit.

A special thanks to everyone who courageously allowed me to write their stories even though they didn't quite know how the book would turn out. This book is for you, it's because of you, and hopefully through your stories, other people will be filled with courage to take steps forward in their own lives.

Thanks to my dad for allowing me to talk about the past. I know others will appreciate the story I've shared because it connects with theirs. I'm so grateful for our relationship today.

Thanks to my small son, who allowed me to write when he really wanted my attention. I love you and I'm always going to love you. I'm so grateful for you.

Thank you to Trevor's mom, who allowed me to write and

dedicate this book to her beloved son. Without your permission, this book would have not been possible.

Special thanks to DWD for helping me to stay inspired. I appreciate the opportunity to be a part of this community.

Thank you to my mentor for sharing your life and family with me. Your song will live in my heart forever.

ABOUT THE AUTHOR

Stephanie Weichert, MBA, ACC, is a certified Life and Executive Coach, Strategic Interventionist, published author and speaker, strategic director for START Fitness®, and business consultant. She has performed life coaching workshops for the Tennessee Army National Guard Warrior Fit Camp program, the Kentucky Army National Guard Operation Immersion course, the Tennessee Army National Guard's Children Attitude Motivation Program (C.A.M.P.), canfitpro in Taiwan and China, and Empower Fitness Conferences. Stephanie is certified as a personal trainer through the National Academy of Sports Medicine (NASM). She has a bachelor's degree from San Francisco State University and an MBA from King University. She has written for magazines and other publications including Military1.com, Military.com, Foundations, Hooah, Military Spouse and GX®: The National Guard Experience.

Stephanieweichert.com

CPSIA information can be obtained
at www.ICGtesting.com
Printed in the USA
LVHW110719141119
637167LV00007B/4/P